D1404998

Through the Year in

ISRAEL

Denise Bergman and Lorna Williams

Batsford Academic and Educational Ltd *London*

Acknowledgments

The Authors would like to acknowledge help from, and give thanks to the following people: Rabbi Broder of the Hull Western Synagogue; Moshe Bar of the Embassy of Israel; The Jewish National Fund Publication Company; Israel Information Centre, Jerusalem; and Mr George Mandel.

The Authors and Publishers would like to thank the following for their kind permission to use copyright illustrations in the book: Israel Government Press Office for the pictures on pages 11, 18, 23 (left), 26, 33 (top); Israel Government Tourist Office, pages 13 (bottom), 24, 36, 38, 53, 60, 63 (right), 68, 69; Israel Labour Archives, page 9 (top); Jewish Agency, page 9 (bottom); A.F. Kersting, page 37; KKL, Israel, pages 15, 30; Wendy Livesey, pages 17, 20 (bottom), 25, 39 (top), 40; Mandel Archive, pages 7 (Robert Laffont), 13 (top left), 19, 21, 23 (right) (Werner Braun), 27, 29, 31, 39 (bottom), 41 (top), 48, 52 (top), 52 (bottom) (Mike Busselle), 54 (David Harris), 55 (top) (Werner Braun), 55 (bottom), 57, 58, 65, 66, 67 (left) (David Harris), 67 (right) (Mike Busselle); Ronald Sheridan's Photo-Library, pages 28, 33 (bottom), 62; Abraham Toren, pages 13 (top right), 43, 44, 63 (left); United Nations, page 10. The pictures on pages 16, 20 (top) and 41 (bottom) are from the authors' collection. The map on page 4 was drawn by Rudolph Britto. The pictures were researched by Patricia Mandel.

Typeset by Tek-Art Ltd, London SE20
and printed in Great Britain by
R.J. Acford
Chichester, Sussex
for the publishers
Batsford Academic and Educational Ltd,
an imprint of B.T. Batsford Ltd,
4 Fitzhardinge Street
London W1H 0AH

ISBN 0 7134 0846 4

Contents

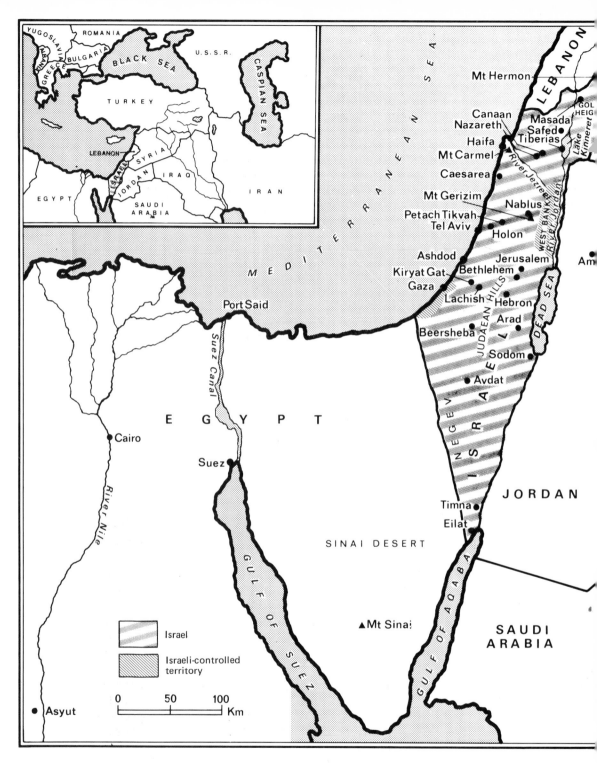

Israel's position in the Middle East.

4

Shalom

Welcome Reader to "Through the Year in Israel". Shalom is one of the most frequently heard words in Israel for, although its literal meaning is "peace", Israelis use it as a friendly greeting when they meet and part. Modern Israel is inseparable from the history of the Holy Land and the Jewish People. Therefore, although the modern State of Israel is less than fifty years old, in order to understand the people and the country today, we must look briefly at the 4,000 years of turbulent colourful history. Part of the excitement of Israel is the great contrast between ancient and modern. Modern technology has made Israel a leading country in many areas — for example, desert technology; while, surrounded by famous biblical sites, one cannot escape the pull of ancient times. It is also an interesting country geographically, as it is located at the cornerstone of three continents — Asia, Europe and Africa. The most fascinating aspect of Israel, however, is the enormous mixture of people of different races, religions and cultures who are learning to live and work together as one nation.

January

The Problem of Time

Time can be expressed in two ways. Firstly, one can choose a moment in time to start counting and then travel forwards. For example, the Christian (Gregorian) calendar starts at the birth of Christ and has so far counted over 1,980 years. The Muslim calendar is counted from the time when the prophet Mohammed (page 66) made his journey from Mecca to Medina, and it reached the year 1400 not very long ago. The Jews, too, have their own calendar, which counts from the time the world is supposed to have been created, and had reached the year 5740 by the beginning of the Gregorian year 1980. Since most of the people who live in Israel are Jews, the Jewish calendar is often used there.

Another method of dating historical events is to take a mid-point and refer to so many years either before or after it. The Christian calendar takes the birth of Christ as this mid-point, and Christians refer to time before this as "Before Christ" (BC) and time after this as "Anno Domini" (AD) — from the year of our Lord. When the Jews, who do not recognize Jesus as Christ (Messiah) or as Lord, refer to the Gregorian year — which is often necessary for practical purposes — many of them prefer to use the phrases "Common Era" (CE) and "Before the Common Era" (BCE) instead of AD and BC.

The Jewish calendar is based on the moon, and a lunar month is the time it takes the moon to travel around the earth. This means that every month in the Jewish calendar begins with a new moon. The beginning of each month is called Rosh Hodesh, and is marked by extra prayers and other ceremonies among observant Jews, in Israel and elsewhere.

A problem is caused by the fact that the solar year – that is, the time it takes the earth to go round the sun – is about 365¼ days, whereas a lunar year, consisting of twelve lunar months, has only 354 days. If the difference of eleven days each year is allowed to accumulate, then dates, such as the first of a particular month, which were once in the spring, would gradually find their way into the winter season. To prevent this from happening, the Jewish calendar has a leap year seven times in each period of nineteen years. A leap year has a whole extra month, which follows the month of Adar and is called Adar Sheni – the second Adar. The next leap year will be 1984 (though, strictly speaking, one should say 1983-84, since the Jewish year 5744 runs from 8 September 1983 to 26 September 1984, and not from 1 January to 31 December) and

after that 1986, 1989, 1992 and 1995 will also be leap years.

In the Gregorian calendar, which is the one most of us are familiar with, all the months (except for February) are made longer than true lunar months, in order to make the number of days in a year come to 365. Even this is a quarter of a day shorter than a true solar year, which is why leap years in this calendar add an extra day every four years. If there were no leap years, then over many hundreds of years Christmas would move from mid-winter to mid-summer, since the seasons are determined by the position of the sun relative to the earth.

In Israel, the Gregorian calendar is used for most everyday purposes, but religious and national festivals are decided according to the Jewish calendar. The Muslim calendar is also widely used, as there are many Muslims in Israel.

In the Beginning

The story of Israel began in about 1700 BCE when God said to Abraham: "Go from your country . . . to the land I will show you" (Genesis 12:1) and Abraham "set forth to go to the land of Canaan". It may seem strange to begin the history of a modern country in the biblical period, but in schools in Israel the Bible is taught as history and children read in it of God's promise to Abraham that the land of Canaan would one day belong to his descendants. To understand the complex situation in Israel today – the mixture of people, traditions, beliefs and modern-day problems, it is necessary to go back to the very beginning and to see out of what circumstances the modern State of Israel was born.

Abraham was the father of Isaac whose son, Jacob, was also called Israel. His descendants are therefore called Children of Israel, or Israelites. During the time of Jacob, a famine in Canaan forced him and his family to settle in Egypt, joining his youngest son, Joseph, who had become a very powerful person after a series of adventures which are related in the biblical book of Genesis. Under a new ruler of Egypt, however, the Israelites were forced into slavery. They were eventually led out of Egypt and their bondage by their greatest leader, Moses, some three or four hundred years after the time of Joseph. For forty years they wandered in the Sinai desert, where they received the Ten Commandments and were taught a new kind of religion — the beginnings of monotheism, the belief in one God.

Finally, under the leadership of Moses' successor, Joshua, they entered the "Promised Land" and, after fierce fighting with the people already living there, who resisted the entry of the Israelites, they settled as farmers and craftsmen. The Land of Israel — as Canaan had now become — was divided among the twelve tribes of Israel and ruled, after Joshua's death, by leaders who were chosen for their powerful personalities and military ability, and who were called Judges — for example, Samson and Gideon.

As a divided land, the country was very vulnerable and for two hundred years suffered many invasions. It was essential to have one ruler and Saul became the first king of Israel. He was succeeded by David in about 1000 BCE and the latter made Jerusalem his capital. David's son, Solomon ruled from 961 to 925 BCE and he is especially famous for the magnificent Temple he built on Mount Moriah in Jerusalem.

When Solomon died, the land was again divided. In the north — Israel, in the south — Judah. The north survived about two hundred years before it was conquered by the Assyrians in 722 BCE. The south survived about three hundred years before it fell to the Babylonians; the Temple was destroyed and the Israelites were exiled. The Babylonians were soon defeated by the Persians and their ruler Cyrus allowed the Israelites to return. It was at this time that the name "Jew" was first used, for the people were called the people of Judah — Jews. Around 520 BCE the Jews began rebuilding the Holy Temple. Persian rule ended when Alexander of Macedon defeated the Persians and brought Greeks to the land. There was a period of calm until, after his death, the

A reconstruction of Herod's Temple, which was destroyed in 70 CE. The nearest wall in the picture is the part which remains today — the "Wailing Wall".

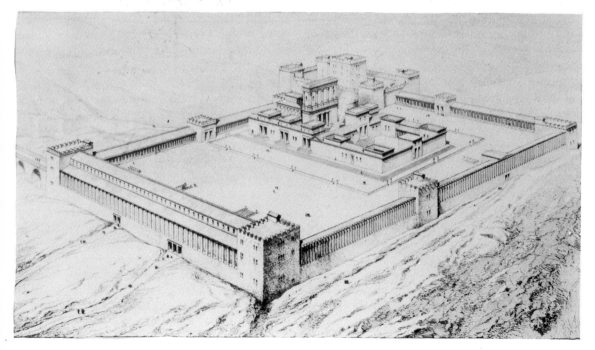

Greeks tried to force their religion and customs on the Jews. Out of this conflict arose the famous Maccabean Rising of 167 BCE, led by Judah Maccabee. Three years later, he and his followers entered Jerusalem, purified the defiled Temple and instituted the eight-day festival of Hanukkah (see page 63).

The next major invading force was Roman. In 63 BCE the Romans, under Pompey, conquered Jerusalem and there followed a period of Roman rule during which time occurred the birth and death of Jesus. Between CE 66 and 73 the Jews rebelled unsuccessfully against Roman rule, the most famous stand taking place at Masada in 72-73 CE (page 00). In 70 CE the Temple in Jerusalem was destroyed for the second time, and has never been rebuilt since.

Between 132 and 135 CE there was another unsuccessful Jewish revolt against the Romans, this one being led by a man named Bar Kokhba. The bitter wars against the Romans led to a great decrease in the Jewish population of Jerusalem and the surrounding district, through death, flight, and enslavement, and for a while Jews were forbidden to enter the city at all. Although some Jews remained in other parts of the country, the great majority now lived abroad, scattered throughout Europe and the Middle East. This settlement of Jews abroad is called the Diaspora, a Greek word meaning dispersion.

With the growth of Christianity, the situation of the Jews left in Palestine — as the Romans called the Land of Israel — grew worse, and many left because of persecution in the fourth century. In the seventh century CE the country was conquered by the Arabs, and Jerusalem, which was already holy to Jews and Christians, became a holy city to yet another religion, Islam (the religion of the Muslims). The famous Islamic shrine, the Dome of the Rock, was built at this time on the site where the Temple had once stood. Soon, the Jews became a small minority in a country whose population was mainly Muslim, and the main centres of Jewish life were in the Diaspora.

Jews did come back to Palestine from time to time, in groups or as individuals, but never in very large numbers — until the twentieth century, that is. They settled in the "holy cities" of Jerusalem, Safed, Tiberias and Hebron, and most of them spent their days in prayer and study, supported by charity from Jews in other countries. In the sixteenth century the Holy Land (as Palestine is often called) was conquered by the Turks and became part of the Ottoman Empire. The new rulers, like their predecessors, were Muslims.

The Birth of a New Nation

In Europe and the other countries of the Diaspora the Jews were a minority. Although they were often under pressure to convert to the religion of the majority (Christianity in Europe, Islam in the Middle East), many resisted and remained stubbornly loyal to their ancestral faith. This made them disliked at times, and the defenceless Jews were often persecuted or attacked by their neighbours, and there were instances of terrible cruelty, with hundreds or thousands of Jewish men, women and children being killed. One such time was in Russia in the 1880s, when there was a series of pogroms (organized massacres). Jews began to flee in large numbers, and although most of them went to the United States, a few decided that, rather than go to yet another country of the Diaspora, they would go to the ancestral homeland, Palestine, and try to live a productive life as their forefathers had done thousands of years ago. These immigrants came to be called the First Aliyah, that is, the first of the waves of Jewish immigration in modern times that led to the establishment of the State of Israel.

These early settlers were exposed to appalling conditions. The Ottoman Administration was hostile; the Jewish population was small, dispersed and had little com-

A group of Jewish settlers on a communal farm at the beginning of the twentieth century.

munication or transport facilities. Malaria and other diseases were common and many people died. Such conditions, however, did not deter the persecuted Jews.

By the late nineteenth century, the Jews in Western Europe believed that antisemitism (page 21) was a thing of the past and that they had been accepted by the countries where they lived. It therefore came as a great shock to them when they realized that antisemitism had merely been simmering under the surface, waiting to rear its ugly head, as it did, for instance, in the Dreyfus trial. In 1894 Alfred Dreyfus, a French Jewish army officer, was falsely accused of spying for Germany. He was later convicted, publicly demoted in a degrading ceremony, and sentenced to life imprisonment on Devil's Island. Even though Dreyfus was later proved innocent and set free, his trial was a very significant event in the history of the modern State of Israel, because of the presence of one man, a Jewish journalist from Vienna, called Theodor Herzl (page 39). Herzl heard the mob crying "Death to the Jews!" and he came to believe that the Jews must leave the countries where they lived, which were infected by incurable antisemitism, and must settle in a land of their own. He organized a Congress of Jews from all over the world in Switzerland in 1897 and founded the World Zionist Organization. (The movement is named after Mount Zion.)

In 1905 a second wave of Jewish immigrants — the "Second Aliyah" — began to arrive in Palestine from Russia. This group came determined to work on the land and to make the soil give forth rich crops, as it had in the past. The Jewish National Fund (page 14) bought land and the immigrants worked on it. In 1909 the first kibbutz (page 42), Degania, was established, and the first

British soldiers of the 3rd Battalion Coldstream Guards entering the old city in 1938, fighting the Arab gangs.

9

defence force, Hashomer, was formed (page 24). By the outbreak of the First World War there were 85,000 Jews in Palestine, reclaiming the land, draining the swamps and bringing life to the soil.

In 1917, with the British occupation of Palestine, the rule of the Ottoman Empire came to an end. 1917 was the year of the famous Balfour Declaration, in which Britain stated publicly that it would regard with favour the establishment of a Jewish Homeland in Palestine. This naturally meant that, with antisemitism on the increase in Europe, many Jews there now chose to go to live in Palestine. Between 1917 and 1948 Palestine was ruled by the British. The history of this period is complex and tragic. Most influential Arabs in Palestine, and in neighbouring countries, were strongly opposed to the Balfour Declaration and to large-scale Jewish immigration, and there were attacks on the Jews in which many of them were killed. The Arabs also put strong pressure on the British to abandon their support of Zionism.

May 1949. The Israeli flag is hoisted as Israel becomes a member of the United Nations.

Years of Conflict

Between 1919 and 1929 the Jewish population increased to 160,000. This meant that there were more people to work on the land and more people to defend the community against Arab attacks, even though Jewish self-defence organizations had to remain underground.

In the late 1930s the likelihood of war between Britain and Germany made the British anxious to keep the strategically-important Arab countries friendly. In 1939, therefore, just as Adolf Hitler in Germany was persecuting Jews savagely, the British announced severe restrictions on the immigration of Jews into Palestine, the very country where Britain had promised them a homeland. An underground immigration movement was formed to help Jews escape to Palestine, but the Royal Navy did its best to intercept ships carrying "illegal" immigrants, and turned many of them away. As relationships between the Jews, the British and the Arabs deteriorated further, Britain eventually took the problem to the United Nations, which recommended, in November 1947, that Palestine be divided into two independent states — an Arab state and a Jewish state. The Arab nations rejected this partition plan and warned that, if Israel proclaimed independence, they would attack the new state and drive the Jews into the sea. On 14 May 1948 the State of Israel was declared, the last British forces left, and the Arab nations declared war on Israel. The Israelis were heavily outnumbered. The new small state was officially fighting Egypt, Transjordan, Syria, Lebanon, Iraq, Saudi Arabia and Yemen (though not all these countries actually took an active part in the war). The Arabs in Palestine began to flee, hoping to return once the war had been won by their allies. However, the badly equipped, 650,000-strong Jewish nation defeated the Arab armies and the war ended early in 1949 with an armistice. The Arab nations refused

JEWISH IMMIGRATION TO ISRAEL 1882-1981		
1st	1882-1903	25,000
2nd	1904-1914	40,000
3rd	1919-1923	30,000
4th	1924-1931	84,000
5th	1932-1938	215,000
6th	1939-1947	154,000
	1948-1970	1,364,991
	1971-1981	355,138

POPULATION GROWTH 1948-1978	
1948	770,000
1951	1,577,823
1954	1,717,814
1957	1,975,954
1961	2,232,300
1965	2,525,600
1969	2,841,100
1971	3,001,400
1978	3,650,800

to sign a peace treaty and Israel retained the territory it had won in the war, making it larger than had been recommended in the United Nations partition plan. The war left Jerusalem a divided city: the western half in Israel, the eastern half, including the site of the Temple, under Arab rule.

Between 500,000 and 750,000 Palestinian Arabs had fled from the area that was now the State of Israel, most of whom were to spend many years living in refugee camps supported by the United Nations. After the war, Jewish immigrants flocked to Israel from every corner of the world. The years 1952-56 were stormy. There were frequent terrorist attacks on Jewish settlements by Arabs from across the borders, and the climax of these tense years was the Sinai Campaign in 1956, when the Israel Defence Forces, commanded by Moshe Dayan (page 24), won a swift victory over Egypt. In 1967 war broke out again, the Israel Defence Forces were once more victorious, and on 7 June they entered the Old City of Jerusalem. For the first time in nineteen years, Jews could pray at the Western Wall, all that remains of the great Temple built by Solomon and Herod.

Blowing the shofar (ram's horn, see page 47) at the "Wailing Wall" in June 1967.

In 1973, on Yom Kippur (see page 49), the holiest day of the Jewish year, Egypt and Syria again attacked Israel. In a series of brilliant military actions the Israeli forces were able to push the enemy back and force them into the defensive. A ceasefire was finally ordered by the United Nations.

The Road to Peace

In 1977 President Anwar Sadat of Egypt paid a State visit to Israel. It was a momentous occasion, as this was the first time an Arab leader had come to Israel accepting the hand of peace. With American help, peace negotiations were opened and on 26 March 1979 a peace treaty was signed by Israel and Egypt.

In 1982, as part of the agreement, Israel handed back the Sinai peninsula, which had been captured from Egypt in the war of 1967. This was giving up a great deal; Sinai contains oil wells, many lives had been lost in gaining the land and many new settlements had been built there. Moreover, by controlling Sinai, the Israelis put several hundred miles of desert between the Egyptian army and their own main centres of population. However, if peace with Egypt proves to be permanent, then the Israelis feel that giving up the land and other assets will have been worthwhile. There is plenty of room in the Middle East for the large Arab countries and one small Jewish nation to live side by side.

February

A Bird's Eye View

The land of Israel is so small that its area could be contained in a 90-mile square. However, travel around the country and you will be amazed by the varied topography. Just as old and new stand side by side in this exciting country, so one finds the extremes of beautiful Mediterranean coast-line, rocky and sandy desert and snow-covered mountains of the north, dominated by Mount Hermon which is a popular ski resort. Travel, for example, a mere half-hour from Jerusalem and you will feel the gradual change of temperature as you leave the city and approach the Negev Desert.

Israel can be divided into three physically different regions: the Coastal Plain; the Hill Region and the Negev; and the Jordan

AVERAGE TEMPERATURES		
	January (°C)	August (°C)
Tel Aviv (Coastal Plain)	11 — 20	22 — 30
Jerusalem (Judean Hills)	5 — 12	19 — 28
Beersheba (Northern Negev)	9 — 20	20 — 30
Eilat (Gulf of Eilat)	11 — 23	20 — 33

Depression. On the west coast, which extends about 120 miles from north to south, are Tel Aviv, Haifa and new towns such as Ashdod. Two thirds of the population of Israel live on this coastal plain which borders the Mediterranean Sea. The soil in this area is rich and used for farming.

Moving eastwards, one approaches the Central Hill Region, with Jerusalem at its

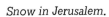
A walk in the rain.

Looking across the Jezreel Valley, past a J.N.F. forest.

Snow in Jerusalem.

```
┌─────────────────────────────────────┐
│                                     │
│     AVERAGE ANNUAL RAINFALL – 1977  │
│                                     │
│                      Cubic Metres   │
│     Coastal Area                    │
│     Nahariya              72.2      │
│     Tel Aviv              59.5      │
│     Ben Gurion Airport    70.8      │
│                                     │
│     Hill Region                     │
│     Jerusalem             65.8      │
│     Beersheba             21.8      │
│     Mt Canaan             72.5      │
│                                     │
│     Jordan Depression               │
│     Eilat (Red Sea)        2.4      │
│     Sodom (Red Sea)        5.8      │
│     Lake Kinneret (Degania) 41.8    │
│                                     │
└─────────────────────────────────────┘
```

of the total area of Israel. It is a dry and desolate landscape of hills and mountains, which receives so little rainfall that it is virtually impossible for any plant life to grow here naturally. Relatively few people live in the Negev and the majority of them are to be found in Beersheba, the main town in the area.

On the eastern border of Israel lies the Jordan Depression. The Jordan Valley is unique because the whole area is below sea level. The River Jordan joins the Dead Sea in this region, which is the lowest point on the earth's surface, some 1,312 feet below sea level.

In a country with such a diverse topography, temperatures and the amount of rainfall vary greatly from area to area. However, generally, one can almost say that there are only two seasons in Israel: winter — from October to April, and summer. The winter is cool and often rainy and there may even be a spell of snow. The summer is always hot and dry.

The Jewish National Fund (J.N.F)

Looking at Israel today, the green fields, the modern towns and mile after mile of cultivated land, it is very hard to believe that at the beginning of the century much of the land was dead and barren. The country was especially bare of trees, due to the periodic wars and invasions of the past 2,000 years. Indeed, the Romans deliberately burned vast areas of woodland, to prevent their enemies from taking cover and hiding in the forests.

The Keren Kayemet le-Yisra'el — J.N.F. — was established at the fifth Zionist Congress in 1901, and it is the body mainly responsible for Israel's new, living landscape. Before independence, the J.N.F.'s main priority was to buy as much land as possible from the Arabs. After 1948 the impetus switched to the cultivation of the land, both for defence and to provide food for the ever-growing stream of immigrants who were flocking to the new State. Jewish people all over the

```
┌─────────────────────────────────────┐
│                                     │
│          FLORA AND FAUNA            │
│                                     │
│   Due to the many different types   │
│   of landscape and the varying      │
│   temperatures, Israel has a        │
│   thriving animal and plant life.   │
│   There are:                        │
│                                     │
│      3,000 types of plants          │
│      400 species of birds           │
│      200 mammals and reptiles       │
│      500 types of tropical fish     │
│         swim in the Gulf of Eilat.  │
│                                     │
│   Israel now has:                   │
│                                     │
│      220 Nature Reserves            │
│      28 National Parks              │
│                                     │
│   In Jerusalem there is a Biblical  │
│   Zoo in which one finds a          │
│   collection of the animals         │
│   referred to in the Bible.         │
│                                     │
└─────────────────────────────────────┘
```

centre. To the north of this chain of mountains, beyond the Jezreel Valley, are the Hills of Galilee, and to the south is the Negev Desert. The Negev covers nearly 60%

The first J.N.F. collecting box, from Herzl's room in the main J.N.F. building, Jerusalem. Many Jewish families had similar boxes, although recently the design has been changed.

trees wherever it could in Israel. Trees prevent erosion and help to create new earth, because, over a period of time, the roots cause the stones to crack and turn into a form of gravel which can then be turned into soil. Trees also have great emotional value. Furthermore, forests act as a counter-measure against pollution; they produce oxygen and absorb dust and harmful gases. The fully grown trees have great economic worth, either as raw material for industry, or as beautiful forests in Israel's National Parks, which attract many nature-loving tourists.

By 1981 over 150 million trees had been planted in Israel — on 560,000 dunams of land (1 dunam = ¼ acre). Once, it was traditional to plant a tree when each new child was born; a cedar for a boy, a cypress for a girl. When the child was grown up and about to marry, "his" or "her" tree would be cut and the timber used for the posts of the Huppah, the canopy under which the marriage ceremony took place (page 41). Today, in Eilat, a new tree is still planted at the birth of each child. Each forest in Israel is given a name. On the Judean Hills stands the Forest of Martyrs — six million trees, each symbolic of a Jewish life lost in Nazi-ruled Europe. Some forests are named after famous people — for example, Herzl, Queen Elizabeth II or Roosevelt. Others may be named after places or concepts, such as "Independence".

There are "Plant a tree with your own hands" centres in Israel, where anyone can go to plant his own tree — though you don't have to go to Israel to take part in this scheme. Donations are sent from all over the world to enable the Israelis to carry on planting new trees, and people receive certificates to say that they have planted a tree in the Holy Land. Trees are often planted to celebrate special occasions, such as a wedding (page 41) or Barmitzvah (page 40).

Tu Bi-Shevat—New Year for Trees

Trees have always been considered of extreme importance in Israel and, each

world have regularly sent voluntary contributions to help the J.N.F. continue its good work. By 1980, with the support of the Diaspora, the J.N.F. had reclaimed over 50,000 acres of land and built over 1,250 miles of road. One famous example of the work of the J.N.F. is the drainage of the Huleh Valley, which was completed in 1958. This area, once a malaria-infested swamp, is now one of the most productive agricultural areas in Israel.

From Small Acorns

The name given to the extensive planting of trees is afforestation and this is a major aspect of land reclamation. From the early days of Zionism, the J.N.F. began planting

February, the Israelis celebrate Tu Bi-Shevat, the New Year for Trees. Throughout the day thousands of trees are planted. For example, in 1982 200,000 saplings were planted all over the country on Tu Bi-Shevat. For the first three years fruit must not be picked from the young trees; in the fourth year the fruit is taken to Jerusalem to be eaten.

Every Hebrew letter has a numerical value (just as do some Roman letters: I, V, X, etc) and the word "Tu" is made up of the two letters that, together, represent the number fifteen: the name of the festival means, simply, the fifteenth of Shevat, which is when it occurs. One of the customs of Tu Bi-Shevat is to taste fifteen kinds of fruit.

Since the date of the festival is decided by the Jewish calendar, it will not always fall in the same month of the Gregorian calendar. As a matter of fact, in 1983 Tu Bi-Shevat did not fall in February but on 29 January. Many of the other festivals mentioned later on in this book under particular months also fall outside those months from time to time; thus, Passover in 1983 began in March, not in April. However, 1983-84 is a leap year, and the extra month (page 6) pushes Passover back to its more usual season.

The Sabra

The sabra, a native fruit of Israel, is a big cactus with flat, prickly leaves and a tough skin. It is sometimes known as a Prickly Pear.

This certificate records the planting of a tree in "Great Britain's Children's Forest" in Israel.

Trees for Israel

Great Britain's Children's Forest

THIS RECORDS THE PLANTING OF

ONE TREE

BY

ROBERT WILLIAMS

IN THE HULI CHILDREN'S GROVE

IYAR 5735   HULI   APRIL '75

JEWISH NATIONAL FUND קרן קימת לישראל

Hard on the outside, it is soft inside and
bears a red fruit. The word sabra is also used
to describe a native-born Israeli — suggesting
that, although the people may seem brash
and arrogant, prickly, on the outside, under-
neath they are really quite sensitive. To the
Englishman, an Israeli may appear pushy,
impatient and inconsiderate; but once you
get to know them, you find sabras very
hospitable.

Travelling Around

If you arrive in Israel from another country,
you may well fly by El Al, Israel's national
airline, and land at Ben Gurion Airport,
which is just outside Tel Aviv. There are
small aeroplanes to take the traveller around
Israel, but most people use the buses, trains
or their own cars. There is a very good road
system linking the major cities, and Egged,
the National Bus Company, provides a cheap
and efficient service.

As well as normal taxis, Israelis can also
choose to use sheruts. Sherut means service,
and a sherut, or "route taxi", does provide a
special service, something between that of a
bus and that of a taxi. It is a car that can
hold up to seven people and it runs along a
fixed route, like a bus — in fact, the route
may well be a bus route, too. Unlike a
private taxi, a sherut goes on selling seats to
anyone who turns up, until none are left. It
costs more than a bus ticket, but the service
may be more comfortable, or faster, or more
frequent. Sheruts also run on the Sabbath,
whereas the state-owned buses do not. There
is also a railway service, but many Israelis
ignore all these possibilities and hitch a lift
instead. Hitch-hiking is an accepted way of
life in Israel and a very common sight along
the roadside are lines of young people, many
in uniform, hitching lifts home.

*The sabra plant, usually known as the "Prickly
Pear".*

17

March

Purim

In March the happy festival of Purim has a dual purpose. Not only does it mark the coming of spring, but it also serves to remind the Israelis of the story of Queen Esther, the second wife of King Ahasuerus of Persia. Before Esther married the King, she lived with her cousin Mordecai, who was a wise and good Jew. Later, Haman, the King's proud and wicked Prime Minister, plotted to have all the Jews in the land killed and it was Queen Esther, prompted by Mordecai, whose risky intervention with the King saved them from this terrible fate.

The Israelis celebrate the festival with street carnivals, and children wear fancy dress and act out the story of Esther. All over Israel, there is outdoor dancing and gaily coloured processions. It is a time of great excitement and festivities. A favourite Purim treat are "Haman's Ears" — little pastry triangles filled with apple and sprinkled with poppy seeds.

Reading the scroll of Esther at Purim, in a synagogue in Tel Aviv. Notice the children in fancy dress.

The Israelis at Home

Housing has always been a problem in Israel because of the large number of immigrants who arrived in a short period of time. In towns people generally live in low-rise multi-storey flats, usually not more than four storeys high. In Jerusalem there are special building regulations which say that all buildings have to be clad in Jerusalem "golden" lime stone, to blend in with the traditional buildings.

Israeli homes are designed to keep the heat and the insects out, while keeping the temperature indoors as cool as possible. The small windows often have mesh screens to keep the flies out, and tiles on the floor help keep the rooms cool. When the Hamsin, the hot dry wind which blows from the desert, begins, the natural reaction is to open windows. But you learn from experience to keep the windows firmly closed, to keep out the hot dry air. Many flats have balconies for drying washing, but washing and cleaning can prove a nightmare, because the climate puts dust, sand and insects everywhere.

18

There are solar panels on the roofs of these apartment blocks in a suburb of Tel Aviv.

Almost everyone has a very large refrigerator which also acts as a pantry and, although the flats are simple and compact, there are many different styles of furnishings. Sabras like modern, simple styles, but the Jews from Africa and India have brought with them more elaborate and colourful furniture.

In the Kitchen

Kashrut is the name given to the preparation, cooking and eating of food according to traditional Jewish dietary laws as found in the Torah (page 55). Because the Jews believed these laws were given by God, they have always followed them, although, today, only the orthodox Jews keep to them fully. Within the rules there is great emphasis on standards of hygiene, health and cattle husbandry. The religious laws still influence Israeli cooking.

Look into an Israeli cookery book and you will find an international cuisine, derived from all the countries in which Jews have lived. It may contain a recipe for blintzes (stuffed pancakes) from Europe; goulash from Hungary; borsht (beetroot soup) from Russia; pickled spicy food from Poland; and curries from India, alongside such traditional dishes as kneidlach (dumplings) and

MEZUZAH

On the front door of Jewish houses, and on the doors of living rooms inside, you will see a Mezuzah. This is a little box which is fastened with nails to the right-hand side of every doorpost of the house. It contains a piece of parchment upon which are written two biblical passages (Deuteronomy 6:4-9 and 11:13-21), each of which contains the verse "And thou shalt write them [the words of God] upon the doorposts of thy house and upon thy gates." On the other side of the parchment is written the Hebrew word for "Almighty", which is visible through an aperture in the box. The Mezuzah is to remind people of God's love and presence. When entering or leaving a room, people usually kiss the Mezuzah by kissing their fingers and touching it with them.

gefilte fish (fish balls). A traditional Israeli breakfast is a true feast, consisting of yoghurt, eggs, tomatoes, salad, bread, cheese, pickles, olives, jam or marmalade, tea or coffee. After this very healthy start, most Israelis have a more Westernized meal at lunchtime — meat or chicken with vegetables are very popular — and a light meal in the evening. This is except for Friday night, when the Shabbat (Sabbath) meal is always specially prepared and served on the best plates, with a fresh clean tablecloth.

Falafel kiosks are to Israel what fish and chip shops are to Britain. Falafel consists of

19

A falafel stall.

savoury fried balls made from chickpeas, served in pitta (Arab bread). This bread has no yeast and is a flat slab shape, which opens up like an envelope waiting to be filled. Together with the falafel, various different types of salad are stuffed into the pitta, making a cheap and filling snack. Tehina, another traditional oriental food, is a paste made from sesame seeds and garlic ground together and usually eaten with pitta or as a dip. Other popular dishes are cholent (a meat stew simmered overnight so that it can be prepared on Friday and eaten hot on the Sabbath), houmus (a spicy paste based on chickpeas) and kreplach (pasta with mince).

Turkish coffee is very popular. It is served hot in tiny cups and is strong, sweet and black. For a longer, more refreshing drink, coffee is served iced, topped with icecream and cream. A popular Israeli nibble is roasted nuts and seeds, and crunching Israelis can be heard on almost every corner!

The Jews

Israel is one of the most cosmopolitan countries in the world. Walk around any city in Israel and you will see people of many races. Step into their homes, smell what's cooking, look at their furnishings and you will quickly realize that the Israelis have come from many different countries and have brought with them a colourful variety of lifestyles. Although the Jewish people share one religion, they have been dispersed all over the world for more than 2,000 years, and each community has adapted itself to the lifestyle of the particular country in which it settled. The links between the Jews in Israel and the Jews in the Diaspora are very strong.

The Jews in Israel can be divided into three main groups. The Ashkenazi Jews came to Israel mainly from Central Europe and

Hasidic Jews at the "Wailing Wall".

				Percentages			
JEWISH POPULATION BY COUNTRY OF ORIGIN							
	1948	*1952*	*1956*	*1960*	*1967*	*1970*	*1978*
Born in Israel	35.4	25.2	32.1	35.9	41.6	46.2	54.2
Born in Asia	8.1	20.6	18.4	16.7	13.3	12.4	20.4
Born in Africa	1.7	7.0	9.6	12.1	14.5	13.9	
Born in Europe and USA	54.8	47.2	39.9	35.7	30.6	27.5	25.4

Russia, and for nearly a thousand years the Jews of these areas spoke a common language, Yiddish. This was originally a Jewish dialect of German (the name comes from "Jüdisch-Deutsch", or Judeo-German), but it developed into a distinct language, written in Hebrew characters. Today, few people still speak it. Within this group one finds descendants of the mystic Polish Jews who have formed their own Hasidic sects. They are easily recognizable by their long dark coats, fur-trimmed hats and pe'ot (side curls).

The second main group are the Sephardi Jews, who are descended from the Jews who lived in Spain. In 1492 they were expelled from Spain and migrated to North Africa, the Balkan countries, Italy, and Turkey, and a small group settled in Safed in Palestine. Their original language was Ladino, or Judeo-Spanish.

The final group of Jews came from Middle Eastern countries such as Syria, Iraq, Yemen and Morocco, and they are called Oriental.

After the Romans had destroyed the Temple, in 70 CE, and the Jews had lost the last vestige of their political independence, they considered themselves as being in exile — an exile that only came to an end with the establishment of the State of Israel in 1948. During the long years of exile the Jews were often treated very badly by the people among whom they lived. Unfortunately,

"Operation Ali Baba", which began in 1951, was similar to "Operation Magic Carpet" (see page 22), and was a massive airlift of 120,000 Jews from Iraq to Israel.

people often feel an unreasonable hatred for small groups who live among them but insist on keeping to their own distinct beliefs or way of life. The Jews have suffered so much from this that there is a special name for the hatred of Jews: antisemitism.

Jews were often expelled from places where they had lived for centuries, or they

21

were treated so harshly that they could not bear to stay in them. In either case, they urgently needed to find new countries to live in and this was often difficult as other countries were not always willing to allow them in. For that reason, one of the first laws passed by the State of Israel was the "Law of Return" (1950), stating that any Jew, from anywhere in the world, had the right to come and live in Israel and become a citizen of the State. During the years up to and immediately after the Declaration of the State of Israel many thousands of immigrants poured into the country by boat, aeroplane and sometimes on foot. They came from places as far away as Australia, Mexico, Argentina, India, the USA and Yugoslavia, but the vast majority came from central Europe and the Arab countries.

There have been Jews in the Yemen for many centuries and tradition says that it was their forefathers who made the decorative doors to King Solomon's Temple; today they are still skilled craftsmen. They had been coming to Palestine in a steady trickle for many years. In 1949 the Israelis mounted "Operation Magic Carpet" and sent aeroplanes to the Yemen to airlift almost all the remaining 45,000 Jews there to Israel. These people had never seen an aeroplane before, but their fears were calmed when they remembered the biblical verse which says that the Children of Israel were borne "on eagles' wings" (Exodus 19:4).

Since the early 1970s there has also been a steady flow of Jews from the U.S.S.R. Although applying for an exit visa may mean great hardship, since it is disapproved of by the Soviet government, many thousands of Russian Jews have persisted in their struggle to leave the country and start a new challenging life in Israel.

The Muslim Arabs

There have always been non-Jewish Israeli citizens, the majority being Sunni Muslim Arabs. During the War of Independence (page 10) many Arabs left Israel, fearing what might happen under a Jewish government. Most of these people have now been living for more than a generation in refugee camps along the West Bank of the Jordan, in Gaza and in Lebanon. However, the Arabs who stayed in 1948 became full citizens of the new State. They have their own religious courts, are equal before the law and are free to observe their own customs and cultural traditions. They have seen a general improvement in their standard of living and benefited from the Israeli education system, health facilities and sanitation programmes. There are many local Arab councils and there are always seven or eight Arab members in the Knesset (Parliament). Arabic is the second official language in the country and there are many books and newspapers in Arabic. Many Arabs are members of the Histadrut (see page 63) and have the same benefits and protection as Jewish Israelis. All non-Jewish Israeli citizens have experienced great changes in the last thirty years. The ties with their traditional way of life have weakened and women have become more independent and have had greatly improved career opportunities.

Against these positive benefits, there are also problems, since Israeli Arabs identify to some degree with their fellow-Arabs in other countries, which maintain a state of war with Israel. Indeed, many have close relations in those countries. Also — which is worse — they are sometimes identified by Israeli Jews with their enemies. Arabs complain that they are often discriminated against and treated as second-class citizens. The situation has become worse since the war of 1967, when Israel's conquest of the area known as the West Bank brought more than half a million additional Arabs under Israeli rule, who are not Israeli citizens. Different Israeli political parties have different ideas on what should be done, and all that can be said with certainty is that finding a solution to this problem is one of the most important and difficult tasks now facing Israel.

April

The Passover

Many Jewish festivals commemorate events we read about in the Bible. The festival of Pesach, the Passover, is one of these, and it normally occurs in the month of April. During the Passover the Jewish people in Israel and the Diaspora remember how Moses led the Children of Israel out of Egypt to the "Promised Land" (page 7). For the whole week of the festival no normal bread may be eaten, only Matzah: unleavened bread. This is to remind the Jews that after God sent the Ten Plagues to Egypt and Pharaoh finally agreed to let the Jewish people go, they had no time to bake ordinary bread — so they made unleavened bread, which can be baked very quickly.

The first night of the Passover is celebrated by a ceremonial meal in the home, called a Seder. The ceremony, which takes place with everyone seated round the table, begins with the youngest son reading a passage from the special Passover book, the Hagadah. The son asks the question: "Why is this night different to all other nights?" The father then reads the Passover story which explains why the festival is celebrated. During the meal there are many symbolic acts. For example, everyone must taste salt-water; this is to remind them of the tears shed by their ancestors during their years of hardship as slaves in Egypt. After the meal the ceremony continues, ending with traditional songs. There are special Seder services in many hotels in Israel, which are filled with Jewish people who have come to the Holy Land especially for the Passover week. Similarly, each kibbutz has its own Seder night service.

It is interesting that, throughout the world, on the first night of the Passover, the Jews in the Diaspora pray: "Next year in Jerusalem." That is, they wish to celebrate the Passover next year living in their home-land. In Israel, however, the prayer is slightly different; the Israelis wish for: "Next year in

An Ashkenazi family gathered round the Seder table at Passover.

Yemenite Jewish immigrants celebrating Passover.

Rebuilt Jerusalem" — meaning Jerusalem with the Holy Temple rebuilt.

The Israel Defence Forces

"With one hand they engaged in the work while the other held the spear"
(Nehemiah 4:11)

The story of David and Goliath, the young shepherd boy defeating the powerful giant, is well-known. The story of modern Israel's survival sometimes seems to be a similar miraculous tale of the small defeating the large, the weak defeating the strong. Excellent leadership and a loyal army have enabled the small state to defeat enemy forces many times larger, and very much better equipped than its own.

The farming settlements set up by Jewish pioneers in Palestine in the late nineteenth century were often attacked by marauding Arab bands. To protect their young settlements, members of the Second Aliyah (page 9) formed a defence force — Hashomer ("The Guard") in 1909. From the outbreak of the First World War in 1914 Hashomer was forced to operate underground. After the war it was disbanded and replaced by Haganah ("Defence"), a large and more representative protection force. Haganah was

an underground organization from the day of its creation. The British — the new rulers of the country, who had driven out the Ottoman Turks in 1917 — had assumed legal responsibility for maintaining peace, and would not sanction independent armed forces. Haganah was created nevertheless, because by 1920 the Jews had come to feel that they could not rely on British protection. Possession of arms was illegal and many Jews, including Moshe Dayan, were imprisoned by the British in Acre Prison for possessing firearms.

During the Second World War, 27,000 Palestinian Jews joined the British Army in

MOSHE DAYAN (1915-1981)

Moshe Dayan was born on 4 May 1915. He was the first child actually to be born on Kibbutz Degania (page 42). His parents were immigrants from Russia, but Moshe was one of the new generation, a sabra. When he was only 14, he joined the Haganah, the secret Jewish defence force, and at 18 he was already a military instructor. He was married in 1935. As a result of underground activity in the Haganah, he spent a period of time in Acre Prison for illegal possession of arms. He lost one eye in 1941 while on a reconnaissance mission in Syria for the British Army and took to wearing the eye-patch that made his appearance famous. He was always extremely self-conscious about the eye-patch and hated people to look at him.

Moshe Dayan had the reputation of being an unconventional, inspiring leader. He commanded the Jerusalem front during the War of Independence in 1948, and in 1953, at the age of 38, he became Chief of Staff (i.e. Commander-in-Chief) of the Israel Defence Forces. When he was appointed, he stated that he intended to change the style and content of the Army, to alter the relationship between himself and the common soldier and to reduce the amount of ceremony. Hence he was known to arrive at bases with no prior warning. His aim was not to "catch out" the commanders of the bases, but merely to remove formality and ceremony. He once said to a young cadet: "Officers of the Israel Army do not send their men into battle. They lead them into battle." He lived by his philosophy and was greatly admired by many people, both soldiers and civilians.

Dayan entered the Knesset in 1959 and in 1967, a few days before the outbreak of war, he was appointed Minister of Defence. After having served as Foreign Minister, too, Dayan died in October 1981.

Moshe Dayan, as Defence Minister.

Men and women soldiers on the Mount of Olives.

fighting against the common enemy. This provided superb training for the eager Jews and many of those who survived were the future leaders of the Israel Army. In 1948, when Israel declared its independence, Israel was attacked simultaneously by several Arab nations. It was during this period that the Haganah and two other underground Jewish military groups joined together to form the Israel Defence Force (I.D.F.), which developed into a well-organized and efficient fighting body.

Everywhere in Israel today you see the light green uniform of the Israeli soldiers. They may be on duty, or merely hitching home from one of the training bases. From age 18, all men must serve three years in the Army, while girls serve 20 months. Then, each year until a man is 55 and a woman is 34 (unless she is married), they must do a month's reserve duty. This ensures that, should the occasion arise, the reserve forces will be prepared. It is considered a great honour to serve in the Israel Army and anyone having served a prison sentence is forbidden to serve in the Force.

Women have the same basic military training as men; they then work in the non-combat areas. They may act, for example, as wireless operators, lorry drivers or nurses. Only in the War of Independence, when the situation was desperate, were women called upon to fight.

Gadna, the voluntary Cadet Force, caters for the 14-18 year olds. This body is under the auspices of both the Ministry of Defence and the Ministry of Education and Culture, for, together with basic military training, it helps integrate the cadets into the broader cultural and social framework of the nation, through such things as education in history and social values, participation in archaeological digs and work in border settlements and immigrant villages. It also helps to re-educate and re-integrate young delinquents.

Having completed basic military training, some soldiers join Nahal, a special corps whose members are trained for life in a pioneering cooperative settlement. They then either go to live on an existing border settlement or establish a new one. Like the early pioneers, they are both cultivating the land and protecting the most vulnerable and dangerous border areas of the country.

25

As the majority of the population have to pass through the machinery of the Army, it serves as an ideal organization for absorbing the immigrants from all over the world into Israeli society. The Army educates its soldiers in the geography and history of Israel. It teaches such subjects as basic mathematics, hygiene and vocational skills which are often useful once the military service is over. And, perhaps the most important, it teaches immigrants the language of their new country.

The Israel Army is not merely a Jewish Army, for there are special units for the Druze, Bedouin and other Arabs who wish to join.

Despite its informal appearance, the Army maintains very high standards in discipline and efficiency. One of its most famous recent exploits was the Entebbe Raid of 1976. Israeli troops were secretly flown to Entebbe airport, in Uganda — more than 2,000 miles from Israel's borders — to rescue Israelis and other Jews who had been kidnapped and were being held there.

The Army takes care to see that those who wish to follow Jewish religious laws while doing military service are able to do so. Army food is always prepared according to the laws of Kashrut, and festivals are observed. For those wishing to continue with their religious studies at the Talmudic Academy, there are the Hesder Units. Soldiers in these units devote their time to both religious study and military service. As a consequence, they may have to serve 4-5 years in the Army.

The role of the Army in Israel extends far beyond that of a mere military institution.

May

Remembrance

May is an emotional month in Israel. The first important day is the Day of the Holocaust, when everyone's thoughts turn to the six million people who were killed by the Nazis during the Second World War simply because they were Jewish. Remembrance services are held in the synagogues.

During the morning a siren is sounded and, as the noise reverberates through the cities, everything stops. Buses and cars stop in the street, the waiter pouring coffee in the restaurant will stop and Israeli Jews stand silently and remember the Jewish people who suffered and died in the concentration camps in Europe. Exactly a week later is Remembrance Day. Again, during the morning, the two-minute siren sounds throughout

Israel, inviting the Israelis to remember those people who gave their lives fighting for their country in the wars against the Arabs. Military services are held all over Israel.

Independence Day

The day after Remembrance Day is a joyful national holiday. It is the anniversary of the signing of the Declaration of Independence. Independence Day has become a day of picnics, especially as everything is closed. Young people spend the day in the open air singing, dancing and eating, while the older generation have their parties at the homes of friends and relatives.

Shavuot

Shavuot is both a religious and an agricultural festival. The word "shavuot" means "weeks" and the festival is celebrated exactly seven weeks after the Passover. The reason for this is that it took the Children of Israel seven weeks to journey from Egypt to Mount Sinai, where Moses received the Ten Commandments from God. Shavuot is called "The Season of the Giving of our Torah". The Torah — the Five Books of Moses — is the most valuable possession Jewish people have and the festival shows their happiness at being chosen to carry out God's laws.

Shavuot is also an agricultural festival celebrated since biblical times. The grain harvest, which started at Passover with the reaping of the barley, came to an end seven weeks later with the harvesting of the wheat, when two loaves of bread, baked from the wheat of the new crop, were offered as a sacrifice. Today Shavuot is celebrated with singing and dancing in the schools and on the kibbutzim, and the synagogues are filled with greenery.

Israeli girls celebrating shavuot.

Lag Ba'Omer

Lag Ba'Omer is a minor festival falling in-between the major festivals, Pesach (Passover) and Shavuot. In ancient times the first sheaf ("omer" in Hebrew) of barley was brought to the Temple as an offering, on the second day of Passover. The seven weeks between that day and the offering of the first wheat, in the form of two loaves of bread, on Shavuot, were a period of semi-mourning among the Jews — for instance, no marriages were permitted during it. The traditional explanation for the mourning is a plague that decimated the disciples of Rabbi Akiva, a great rabbi of the second century CE. The 33rd day of this period, however, when the plague is said to have lifted, is treated as a holiday. Three-year-old boys are given their first haircut (haircuts are forbidden during the rest of the Omer period), and bonfires are lit. The day is called Lag Ba'Omer — "Lag" means 33, from the numerical values of the letters that make the word (see page 16).

The Dead Sea Scrolls

In 1947 an Arab shepherd boy looking for his sheep came across some jars containing scrolls of parchment or papyrus, in a cave on the northwest shore of the Dead Sea. These turned out to be very ancient Hebrew texts, including some of the books of the Bible, which had belonged to a Jewish sect living in the region in the Second Temple period. In succeeding years more manuscripts were found in other places along the western side of the Dead Sea, including some letters from Bar Kokhba (page 8), together with skeletons, linen, remnants of clothes and other domestic objects connected with his revolt. Many of these documents and other objects are now in a museum in Jerusalem

The Shrine of the Book, Jerusalem. This museum houses many of the Dead Sea Scrolls, and is designed in the shape of the top of the container in which the scrolls were found. The museum also houses the Bar Kokhba letters and the things found with them.

called the Shrine of the Book. The manuscripts found in various places near the Dead Sea, written at different times by different people, are referred to together as the Dead Sea Scrolls.

The Salty Sea that is really a Lake

The Dead Sea, which is really a large lake, is 50 miles long and 10 miles wide. As it is eight times as salty as ordinary sea water, it is impossible for anyone to sink in it. It is also too salty for any fish to survive, but the salt and minerals present provide the basis for a thriving chemical industry. The sulphurous springs around the Dead Sea are very good for treating skin diseases and rheumatism.

ARAD

Arad is a modern town, built since 1962 to provide a work force for the chemical industry based around the Dead Sea. It rises dramatically out of the desert, and the warm, dry, pollen-free air is ideal for asthma sufferers. It is named after the biblical city of Arad 6 miles to the west, which was excavated by Israeli archaeologists between 1962 and 1967.

The Judean Desert.

Sodom, on the edge of the lake, was a wicked city full of vice. The Bible tells us how, nearly 4,000 years ago, God allowed Lot — the nephew of Abraham — and his family to escape from the city before He destroyed it. But they were told not to look back at the city while it was being destroyed. Lot's wife disobeyed this order, and was turned into a pillar of salt. Every local bus driver now has his own particular pillar, which he points out as being this unfortunate lady. The whole area is full of many strange salt formations caused by evaporation and erosion. The level of the Dead Sea is steadily dropping because of evaporation, and planners are considering either a pipeline from the Mediterranean to the Dead Sea or even the possibility of building a canal from the Mediterranean coast to the Dead Sea.

The Judean Desert

Between the Qumran Caves in the north, where the first Dead Sea Scrolls were found, and Sodom in the south lies the ancient fortress of Masada (page 59). From Masada

BEN GURION (1886-1973)

David Josef Green was born in Plonsk, Russia in 1886. The family lived quite a comfortable life, but David was a rather weak and sickly child. His mother died when he was 11 and for a time he withdrew very much into himself. He was taught Hebrew by his grandfather, while his father sowed the seeds of his love for the Land of Israel. At an early age he took Herzl as his hero and he decided that he must live in Palestine. From the age of 14 he became very involved with Zionist activities and from 1905 he was an active member of Po'alei Zion — "Workers of Zion", the Zionist Labour Movement. In 1906 he emigrated to Palestine where he took the Hebrew name of David Ben Gurion.

On arriving in Palestine, for a period of time he worked on the land. Then he entered the world of politics. He married in 1917, but this marriage always took second place to his work and devotion to the country. Between 1921-35 he served as the General Secretary of the Histadrut (the General Federation of Labour). There were few modern hospitals and roads in Palestine at that time, and Ben Gurion and the early settlers worked all hours of the day and night to build their new country.

In 1947 Ben Gurion became responsible for the Defence of the Jewish community. In his usual thorough way, he read, questioned and researched until he was well-grounded in every aspect of military planning. It was Ben Gurion who was largely responsible for the organization and modernization of the Israel Army. On 14 May 1948, as head of the Jewish Provisional Government, he proclaimed the existence of the Jewish State and announced that it would be called the State of Israel. He then became Israel's first Prime Minister. Thus, Herzl's dream was realized and Ben Gurion, his disciple, was greatly responsible for making the dream come true. During the 1948 war Ben Gurion was both Prime Minister and Minister of Defence.

After the war immigrants flocked to Israel and Ben Gurion aimed to double the population within four years. This meant vast schemes to provide homes, food and education for the new immigrants. The target was reached; immigration became an established routine and Ben Gurion was tired. He had achieved his aims for the country; for the time being, things were running smoothly and he desperately required a rest. So in 1953 he resigned and settled on Kibbutz Sedeh Boker in the Negev.

His move to the Negev desert was a deliberate action to encourage others to leave the heavily-populated central areas of the country and follow him to the nearly-empty Negev, returning to the pioneering ideals of the early Zionist settlers. Once again he was working on the land. He grew healthier, tanned and more relaxed, despite the visitors he received every day.

In 1955 he returned to political life as Defence Minister and held the premiership during the 1956 war. He resigned in 1963 and died ten years later on 1 December. He was buried at Sedeh Boker, next to his wife.

David Ben Gurion chairing a meeting, beneath the portrait of his hero.

to Beersheba you cross exciting desert terrain. One moment there are jagged boulders and the next there are huge rocks and ridges dramatically rising out of the earth. The colours in the desert are soft pinks and rich purples as the sun slowly crosses this inhospitable countryside. The Negev desert has a rugged beauty and as the area has less than 20 days of rain per year it lives up to its name, as Negev means dry. This part of Israel is full of associations with the biblical era. Abraham and Isaac dug wells there. Today, Beersheba is known as the Capital of the Negev and it has undergone very rapid growth in the last 30 years. The population has increased from 2,000 in 1948 to over 100,000 today. Immigrants have settled here from all over the world and there are several institutes of research into desert technology.

The Travelling Bedouin

The Bedouin are desert nomads who for centuries have been coming to market at Beersheba to sell their animals and woven cloth, to shop and exchange news and gossip. Their traditional lifestyle is now changing though, and many Bedouin have settled permanently in Beersheba and have jobs in factories. Others continue more traditional occupations but use motorbikes and trucks instead of camels! Although it may seem a pity to lose such a unique way of life, the Bedouin have greatly benefited from Israel's modern health and social welfare schemes.

Making the Desert Bloom

One of Israel's greatest challenges is lack of water. Hard-working and enthusiastic farmers have turned parts of the Negev from parched desert to green and fertile land. Irrigation is a perennial problem in Israel and, as water is so very precious, the normal sprinkler or ditch methods of irrigation are considered too wasteful. The Israelis have a method of

The National Water Carrier, carrying the water from the north of Israel to irrigate the south.

using plastic piping which has holes in it, enabling the farmers to regulate exactly how much water is used. The desert farmers also use plastic sheeting for protecting young plants from the burning sun or, surprisingly even in the desert, from frost.

Most of the water for irrigating the thirsty south comes from the north of Israel. The National Water Carrier Pipeline was completed in 1964 and it carries water from Lake Kinneret (the Sea of Galilee) through pipes, aqueducts, canals, artificial reservoirs, tunnels and dams to the Negev. Research is also going on into other possibilities, such as using recycled sewage water, desalinating sea water and seeding clouds to make the rain start falling. The people of the Judean and Negev desert regions may have their geographical roots firmly fixed in the past but, as far as living and working in the desert is concerned, their outlook is most definitely towards the future.

31

Governing Israel

The political life in Israel has always been a lively affair, with very many political parties covering the whole political and religious spectrum. In fact, no party has ever won an outright majority and governments are formed by parties working together in a coalition.

The Knesset is the name of the Parliament and it chooses a President to act as Israel's Head of State. This role is similar to the Queen's in Britain. The President performs mainly ceremonial duties such as signing laws and representing the country. The first President to be elected was Chaim Weizmann, a scientist, who had been one of the people chiefly responsible for obtaining the Balfour Declaration from Britain in 1917, and who had led the Zionist movement for most of the time since then.

All Israelis are eligible to vote at 18, and they cast their votes for a political party rather than for an individual candidate. 120 members are elected by a system of proportional representation. This means that each party receives a number of seats in proportion to the number of votes it gains.

The Knesset sits for four years. There is always much discussion over the question of how much of Jewish religious law should be incorporated into the law of the State. Although the members usually debate in Hebrew, they may also address the House in Arabic.

June

Leisure Time

One would not expect that a country, which has always felt the need to fight for its very existence, would have much time to devote to the arts. However, even during periods of intense persecution, the Jews have striven to keep cultural activities alive. Survival is not enough; the finer things in life must survive too.

Making Music

The study of music is very popular in Israel. There are many choirs, school orchestras and music students. Contemporary music is varied, reflecting the rhythms and themes of both Eastern and Western civilizations. Western pop music is widely played and the Israelis have a strong popular music tradition of their own. Classical music has a large following and jazz and other types are enjoyed too. Winning the Eurovision Song Contest in 1978 and being runners-up in 1983 were exciting events for the Israelis. The famous Israeli Philharmonic Orchestra, founded in 1936, presents 230 concerts at home each year, in addition to its many successful overseas tours. The Ein Gev Musical Festival, a major popular musical event which takes place each spring on the shores of Lake Kinneret, attracts thousands of people.

Drama

Israel boasts five major theatrical companies. They are based in the large towns but tour

The Habima Theatre.

The Roman amphitheatre at Caesarea.

frequently, presenting Western plays, classical plays and new Hebrew works. The Haifa theatre group is especially famous for works portraying current problems and general life in Israel. The most dramatic setting for both drama and music is the Roman Amphitheatre at Caesarea. Once the arena was used for gladiatorial contests. 1,700 years later, it is used for concerts and plays throughout the summer months. The first modern performance took place there in 1961. Microphones do not have to be used because the light sea breezes from the Mediterranean carry the songs and music inland to the audience.

The very landscape and history of the country have helped the development of a film industry, for Israel provides a ready-made background for films based on the Bible. The Israeli film industry produces about 20 films a year. The first television broadcast was in 1968 and now there are both Hebrew and Arabic programmes. Approximately half of the total programmes shown are educational.

The national radio, Kol Yisra'el (The Voice of Israel), broadcasts in Hebrew, Yiddish, English, French, Russian, Persian and other languages. News is reported each hour. In addition there is an independent offshore station called "Abie Nathan's Voice of Peace". This transmits to Israel and the Arab countries, in Hebrew, Arabic and English, and presents "Peace Talk Shows" 24 hours a day.

Fact and Fiction

The Israelis are avid readers. Twelve million books are published annually and Tel Aviv is quoted as having more bookshops per head than any other city in the world. There are 750 public libraries in Israel and a fifth of the population are members. Indeed, twelve new libraries have been built in Jerusalem in the past twenty years, several being devoted purely to works in Arabic.

The Israelis are said to read more newspapers per head than any other country. They have a vast choice of papers, for, as the population is so mixed, the media must cater both for all levels and for all languages. Consequently, there are Hebrew and Arabic dailies, special papers in easy Hebrew for the immigrants, and papers in at least a dozen other languages.

Two Left Feet!

Dancing has always been popular with Jewish people all over the world and in Israel this traditional love of dancing continues. Israel's folk dancing combines the music and rhythms of many different countries, and the Hora — a dance chiefly of Rumanian origin — is so popular that it has practically become the national dance of Israel. Like many Israeli dances, the Hora is danced not in couples but by the whole group formed into a circle, suggesting unity. The music starts slowly, and gradually becomes faster, reaching an exciting climax.

Women

There is no stereotype Israeli woman. One may see an Israeli woman walking up the street in army uniform; working on a kibbutz; or living in a Bedouin tent serving her husband. The women in Israel belong to many different races and cultures; and these determine how they dress, the type of food they may cook and the roles they play within the community. The Israeli Declaration of Independence states that Israel will "maintain complete equality of social and political rights for all its citizens without distinction of creed, race or *sex*." Theoretically, all women in Israel, regardless of their race or religion, have equal opportunities with men to follow their careers and develop their own personalities. This may be true in practice in some areas of the community. However, often, among both Muslim Arabs and orthodox Jews, deep-rooted customs and religious beliefs tend to confine women to traditional domestic roles.

HANNAH SZENES (1921-1944)

Hannah Szenes was a Hungarian Jewish immigrant who arrived in Palestine in 1939. She worked on several agricultural settlements and in 1944 volunteered for the British Army, to be parachuted back into Hungary to try to help European Jews, who were suffering under Nazi persecution. She was caught, imprisoned, tortured and later executed as a British spy. She showed outstanding courage and is remembered in Israel as a modern heroine. During her short life she showed great literary ability and her poetry and writings are familiar readings in Israeli schools. Several dozen streets, two farming settlements, a ship and a forest have been named after her. In 1950 her remains were taken to Israel and reburied in a special section of the National Military Cemetery in Jerusalem.

Harvest

Our people are working the black soil,
Their arms reap the gold sheaves,
And now when the last ear its stalk leaves
Our faces glitter as with gilded oil.

From where comes the new light and voice,
From where the resounding song at hand?
From where the fighting spirit and new faith?
From you, fertile Emek*, from you, my land.

*Emek — valley, namely The Valley of Jezreel

Written in Nahalal, 1940 and translated by Peter Hay; from *Hannah Senesh: Her Life and Diary* (1971) by Vallentine Mitchell, London, translated by Marta Cohn

The words of Theodor Herzl in 1897 may explain why Israeli women were encouraged from the outset to develop their talents. He wrote that "A nation striving to be recognized as equal among other nations can ill afford not to recognize women as equal among men." Indeed, it was both necessity and their own determination which made the first women settlers work on the land alongside their menfolk, and similarly, during times of trouble, they fought side by side against the enemy.

Today there is compulsory military service for Jewish women, except for some from strictly orthodox families who object on religious grounds to their daughters serving in the Army. The kibbutz environment encourages equal division of labour between the sexes, for the task of caring for all the children in the community is allotted to a certain number of people, thus leaving the mothers generally free to participate in kibbutz work. In the city, a working mother is aided by the existence of creche facilities, where she may leave her child in safe hands while she goes to work.

Women have always taken an active part in the country's political life. In the first Knesset of 1949 almost 10 per cent of the members were women, including Golda Meir who was later to be Israel's first woman Prime Minister. Women also play an active part in the arts world. For example, there are women painters, conductors and musicians, while women have played the leading part in setting up ballet schools and dance companies in Israel.

W.I.Z.O.

The Women's International Zionist Organization (W.I.Z.O.) was founded in 1920, with the aim of helping women in Palestine: equipping them to serve the needs of the country and supporting them in their personal needs. At first, schools were established providing training in agriculture and domestic science, but after the Second World War, with the large influx of immigrants, the aims and work of W.I.Z.O. expanded. It provided training in both vocational and domestic areas: for instance, farming, typing, photography, cooking, hygiene, child care and sewing. It established women's hostels and gave financial and moral support to young female immigrants.

Today W.I.Z.O. is an extremely strong

GOLDA MEIR (1898-1979)

Golda Meir was born in a Jewish Ghetto in Kiev in Russia on 3 May 1898. When she was still a child, her family emigrated to America. They were extremely poor and often short of food. Golda trained to be a teacher and became an active member of the Zionist Movement. She married Morris Myerson who was also from Russia, and in 1921 they made the big decision to emigrate to Palestine. It took quite a while for Golda to prove herself to the other members of the kibbutz which they had joined, but eventually she was accepted by the other kibbutzniks. Unfortunately, her husband suffered from bad health and they were forced to leave the kibbutz.

Conditions in Palestine at this time were hard and it was virtually impossible to find work. The Myersons now had two children, a son and a daughter, and life was very difficult for them. Golda had joined the Labour Movement in the United States and was also active in the World Zionist Movement. Her great energy, enthusiasm and her sincere and persuasive way of speaking brought her more and more into political life and in 1948 she was one of the people who signed Israel's Declaration of Independence. She served as Israel's first Ambassador to the Soviet Union, and was elected to the Knesset in Israel's first elections, in 1949.

She held various posts in the Knesset. Prime Minister David Ben Gurion made her Minister of Labour in 1949 and she was later Israel's Foreign Minister for nine years. Ater her husband's death in 1956, she hebraicized her name to Meir. In 1969, when Prime Minister Levi Eshkol died in office, Golda was brought from retirement, at the age of 70, to be Israel's new Prime Minister.

Ben Gurion had called her "the only man in my Cabinet" because she supported his tough policy towards the Arab countries. She had almost superhuman energy and a powerful charisma. She served as Prime Minister during five very tense and difficult years which included the "Yom Kippur" war of October 1973 (page 12). Golda Meir died in February 1979.

Golda Meir with Dr Henry Kissinger, United States Secretary of State.

body with organizations in most countries of the world which send aid and support to the women and children in Israel. There are now 180 clubs and centres for women in Israel. These provide counselling on such subjects as women's rights and employment. Monthly seminars on current events help make women aware of what is happening in the country and therefore enable them to actively participate in the life of the country. W.I.Z.O. has also established clubs for the Arab and Druze women in Israel.

July

Jerusalem the Golden and the Fast of Tammuz

Jerusalem is a city shrouded in mystery. One moment you can be walking down a twentieth-century modern avenue with department stores, hear people discussing current problems and see the latest fashions. Turn a corner into old Jerusalem and you find yourself in an oriental market which seems to have changed very little for hundreds of years.

One of the days remembered by Jews as a great disaster in their history is the seventeenth day of Tammuz of the year 70 CE. It was then that the Roman armies, commanded by Titus, first succeeded in breaching the walls of Jerusalem. More than 600 years earlier, when Nebuchadnezzar had besieged the city, he, too, first succeeded in breaching the walls during the month of Tammuz. Both of these events are commemorated on 17 Tammuz, when Jews everywhere fast and say special penitential prayers in the synagogues.

The only part of the Temple that remained after the year 70 was the Western Wall,

Jerusalem, viewed from the Mount of Olives. In the centre of the picture is the Temple area. The Dome of the Rock is on the right, and the dome of the Mosque of Aksa on the left.

Praying at the "Wailing Wall".

which can still be seen today. With its close links with the past, this wall has become a very special place at which to worship. Tradition says that, if you write your prayer on a piece of paper, push it into a crevice in the Wall and then pray, your prayer will be answered. When Jerusalem was united in 1967, Moshe Dayan, the Minister of Defence, was one of the first people to do this. He wrote: "May peace descend upon the whole House of Israel."

Christians have come to call the wall the "Wailing Wall", having seen how, for centuries, Jews came there to lament over the destruction of their Temple.

During the Jews' long exile from the Holy Land, Jerusalem always remained close to their hearts. To ensure that the vow taken "by the Rivers of Babylon", not to forget Jerusalem — "If I forget, thee, O Jerusalem, may my right hand wither" (Psalm 137:5) —

was kept, several references to the city were inserted into the prayers that Jews say three times every day.

When the War of Independence ended early in 1949, part of Jerusalem was controlled by the Arab Legion, the other half by the Israeli Army. The result was that, from then until 1967 Jerusalem was a divided city, with part belonging to Jordan and the rest to Israel. The Old City and many Jewish holy places were in the Jordanian half, to which the Israelis were denied access. However, in 1967, during the Six Day War, Israeli troops captured the Jordanian half and, after the war, knocked down the dividing wall and reunited the city. Today, all places of interest are open to all visitors, irrespective of race, religion or nationality. Jerusalem is Israel's

Old and new in Jerusalem.

words "ir" meaning "city" and "shalom" meaning "peace", one hopes that the "city of peace" can now live up to its name.

Jerusalem is not a major centre for shopping or commerce and has none of the dazzling "bright light" feeling of bustling Tel Aviv. People visit Jerusalem to admire the beauty of the buildings and landscape, to relive the great historical events and for the sense of holiness that the city exudes. There is an old Jewish saying that God gave the world ten measures of beauty; nine fell on Jerusalem and the other one on the rest of the world. This is easy to understand when you see the Jerusalem stone glowing golden in the sunlight or giving off a silvery sheen in the moonlight.

The Old City of Jerusalem is surrounded by tall thick walls which were built over 400

capital and, as the name is traditionally explained as deriving from the Hebrew

---

THEODOR HERZL (1860-1904)

Theodor Herzl was born in Budapest in Hungary on 2 May 1860. When he was 19, his family moved to Vienna and Herzl began to study law. But very soon he decided to give this up and devote himself to writing. He had received some Jewish education, both at school and at home, but he became very aware of his Jewish identity only when, in his early youth, he encountered antisemitism in Vienna and abroad.

His book *The Jewish State* was published in 1896. In it, he analysed the Jewish Problem and decided that the only solution to the plight of the Jews was for them to find a land of their own and set up a Jewish State there. In 1902 he wrote his utopian novel describing how he imagined Palestine in the future, after it had become a Jewish State. He called his work *Altneuland* "Old-New-Land"; old, because it was the ancient homeland of the Jews; new, because it would be the land of a new Jewish State. On the title page were the words: "If you will it, it is no dream," and these words became the inspiration of the Zionist Movement, a movement which took its name from Mount Zion in Jerusalem, whose name had become symbolic of the entire Holy Land.

Herzl died in July 1904. Soon after the State of Israel came into existence, his body was brought from Vienna to Jerusalem and reburied there, on a hill that is named after him — Mount Herzl. The anniversary of his death, 20 Tammuz, was declared a national day of memorial in Israel, for Theodor Herzl is regarded as the Father of Political Zionism.

The Father of modern Israel.

A sign at the entrance to the Meah Shearim district of Jerusalem.

years ago by Suleiman the Magnificent, a Turkish Sultan. At regular intervals in the wall there are seven gates with appropriate names: for example, Lions Gate has stone lions at either side and Dung Gate used to lead out onto the refuse tip. Within the walls lie the four traditional quarters: the Christian, Armenian, Muslim and Jewish areas. Today, however, most of the very orthodox Jews live outside the Old City, in the district of Meah Shearim.

Jerusalem has faced many crises in the past. Today the problem is how to reconcile the demands for twentieth-century living, working and leisure with the wish to preserve the historical buildings and the character of the city.

Coming of Age

Until a boy is 13 years old, Jewish law considers that his behaviour is the responsibility of his father. From the age of 13 and a day, however, he is legally and morally responsible for his own actions and Jews mark the occasion by a ceremony called Barmitzvah — literally, "Son of a Commandment", meaning that the boy is subject to all the commandments of the Torah. On the first Sabbath after his thirteenth birthday, at the time when a section of the Torah is always read aloud in the synagogue, the boy is called up to the platform and he himself reads all or part of the section, to the traditional chant. He also reads the Haftarah, the passage from one of the books of the Prophets which always follows the reading from the Torah on a Sabbath. He is then considered an adult member of the community and can, for instance, be counted in a "minyan" — the quorum of ten adult males which is necessary for communal prayer to take place.

A girl is considered to have come of age legally when she is 12 and a day, and from the nineteenth century the custom has spread of having a coming-of-age ceremony for girls, too, called Batmitzvah — "Daughter of a Commandment". Barmitzvahs and Batmitzvahs are also marked by parties and family celebrations, and gifts for the boy or girl.

40

A Barmitzvah ceremony on the summit of Masada.

A Jewish Wedding

In Israel, as elsewhere, different religious groups have different ceremonies and traditions for joining two people together in marriage. All Jewish weddings follow a similar pattern, based on ancient traditions, but differences occur between, for instance, Sephardi and Ashkenazi Jews, and between the less and the more orthodox. Perhaps surprisingly, the celebrations of a very religious couple would be far more informal than the more restrained celebrations of the less religious.

The very religious couple follow all laws leading to their wedding day. They do not see each other for seven days before the wedding. Then, when the great day arrives, it is customary for both bride and groom to fast, so their sins may be forgiven. Even at the hall where the service and celebrations are to take place, they must not meet. The bride, who is regarded as a queen, sits on a chair covered with a white cloth and greets her guests, who, by tradition, tell her how beautiful she looks, while the groom must greet the guests in another room.

Eventually, the groom is escorted to his bride by the two fathers. He must look at his bride to check that she is the right woman. This custom became part of the marriage service in remembrance of how, in the Bible story, Jacob found that he had married Leah instead of her sister Rachel, the woman he loved. The bride's face was covered by a veil, and the girls' father had made use of this fact to trick Jacob into marrying Leah, the older and less attractive of his two daughters. After this, the bride and groom are taken outside for the ceremony, which takes place under the Huppah or bridal canopy, a cloth (sometimes a prayer-shawl), held up by four poles. The groom and some witnesses sign a marriage contract. A dramatic part of the ceremony is when the groom smashes a glass by stamping on it. This is to remind the couple and all present that all is not well, even at this happy occasion, for the Great Temple is still in ruin.

Once the ceremony is over, the bride and groom, accompanied by much singing, go into a separate room to break their fast alone together. Then there is great rejoicing.

Celebrating a Jewish wedding in Jerusalem.

41

The bride must not dance with her husband, but she leads the women in a series of excited wild dances, while the groom dances madly with his friends.

Finally, it is time for food which is followed by grace after meals. After the grace, seven male friends of the couple recite seven special wedding blessings, and it is traditional on the seven nights following the wedding for the young couple to be entertained at seven friends' houses, with food, song and discussion.

August

The Kibbutz

The kibbutz is a way of living unique to Israel. The word "kibbutz" means "group".

In 1909 seven young pioneers, recently arrived from Europe, set up a farm which they called "Degania" ("Cornflower"), on a plot of land belonging to the Jewish National Fund (page 14). The seven had previously worked on another farm owned by the J.N.F. where they had been on bad terms with the farm administrator, and they wanted their new farm to be run communally, with everyone having an equal say in making decisions. Living conditions were harsh, as the land was full of swamps, with dangerous malarial mosquitoes causing many deaths. The pioneers lived in tents, with no electricity or plumbing, and with very limited financial resources. It turned out that sharing all that they had and working together as a group made better sense economically than trying to farm individually. Other, like-minded, settlers arrived at Degania, and gradually the principles of collective settlement began to be worked out. One of them was that the women played an equal part. In the years that followed, when children came along, some of the women made it their responsibility to look after all the children, thus freeing the other women for farming.

This was the beginning of the kibbutz movement. Today, there are about 230 kibbutz villages ("kibbutzim"), housing 101,600 people (1980). The kibbutzim vary in size from 200 to 2,000 people, but the main theme is still the communal ownership and the collective planning and running of the kibbutz. Every member over 18 has a vote, enabling him or her to participate in a weekly general assembly which forms the basis for kibbutz democracy. The assembly elects office holders — for example, Farm Manager, Works Organizer — and also discusses problems relating to education, health, housing and leisure on the kibbutz. All work is shared, including agricultural work, the laundry, cooking, cleaning and child rearing — and equal value is placed on all kinds of work.

Immediately after birth, a kibbutz child is normally placed in the Children's House. The mother visits her young baby there frequently for feeding, but once it is weaned, she returns to work and leaves the baby in the capable hands of the "metapelet" (nanny). In most kibbutzim the children all live together in one house. They grow up with children of a similar age to themselves and develop strong emotional bonds with these friends. They eat, sleep, play and have their elementary education in the Children's House and, although their parents can visit them at any time during the day, there is also a fixed time in the afternoon, after the parents finish work, when the children visit their parents' houses. Many kibbutzim have children's farms with small livestock such as chickens and goats, for which the children are responsible. The older children also have committee meetings to discuss any matters concerning their house and so, from a very early age, the children are learning about sharing and co-operating.

Once the children reach their teens, they attend a secondary school on one of the kibbutzim in the region which belongs to the same kibbutz movement as their own. Here, the children from many kibbutzim meet. After school each day, the growing adolescent is expected to do some work on his own kibbutz. The work load gradually increases as the teenagers mature until, by the time they are 18, they are making a valuable contribution to their community and at the same time feeling that they are important members of the team.

At 18, all young people are called up to serve in the Israel Defence Forces (page 24). Afterwards, if a person has the ability and the desire to study, the kibbutz may sponsor

In the kitchen on the kibbutz.

him or her at a college or university. On returning home, the former kibbutz child is invited to become a member of the kibbutz. About 75% of kibbutz-born children decide to become members. The rest leave, usually to settle in one of the towns and lead a more independent life.

At one time there was a strong tendency in the kibbutz movement to downgrade the importance of the family, compared with the community, but in recent years there has been a reaction against this. It is still true that the kibbutz performs many of the functions which elsewhere are the jobs of the family. The mother and father are not the breadwinners and do not provide the food, toys and clothes for the children. It is not the parents' job to discipline or make decisions for the children. These things are done communally by all kibbutz members. But in recent years there has been growing opposition to having the young children sleep away from their parents, and in some kibbutzim it is now the rule for them to sleep at home.

Kibbutz members usually have their own living accommodation but take most of their meals in a common dining-hall, and often read newspapers and watch television together in the kibbutz club rather than in private. The accommodation may be a room in a primitive wooden hut, for a young unmarried member, or a well-built house, for a married couple. The houses are small, but nowadays usually have a kitchen so that the couple can, if they wish to, eat alone together rather than in the communal hall. Often they will have their midday meal in the hall and their evening meal at home.

On a kibbutz, all a person's material needs are taken care of, from birth to death, without any exchange of money. Members do not own anything individually except personal items of little value. Each member has a personal allowance, a notional amount of money, which he can "spend" at the kibbutz shop, which has a vast selection of goods. The kibbutz movement was founded on the

Taking the children for a walk.

The children's farm at the kibbutz.

principle, "from each according to ability; to each according to his need", meaning, for instance, that a disabled person who cannot work very hard is still entitled to have everything provided, and that the strongest and most tireless member gets no more reward for his efforts than anyone else.

A working day starts early, at sunrise. Although, originally, the kibbutz was solely agricultural, recently many have developed light industrial plants, making furniture, electronic parts and precision tools, alongside the more traditional poultry farming, fruit orchards, fish farms, olive groves, vineyards and arable farming. Only about 3% of Israelis live on a kibbutz, but they produce about 40% of the whole country's agricultural output and about 7% of the industrial exports. Many kibbutzim have also entered the tourist trade, by providing guest house accommodation for visitors.

As a person grows older, the length of his working day gradually decreases. In this way, old people still contribute a little and the kibbutz allows a gradual retirement and thereafter provides a warm caring environment for the elderly.

The kibbutz movement is subdivided into several different organizations, which differ along political and religious lines. Some movements are very left-wing (these are usually anti-religious); others are very orthodox in religion; or simply more middle-of-the-road politically. They may differ slightly on the degree of communal living; for example, in one organization, it may be common for children to sleep in their parents' house and, in another, the children may live completely in the Children's House. These differences are frequently debated vociferously within the kibbutz movements.

Despite over seventy successful years, the kibbutz movement is not without its problems. The very closeness of communal living can create tension, and some people find it difficult to cope with the lack of privacy and autonomy. Personal housing is usually a low priority when establishing a kibbutz, so

living accommodation often leaves much to be desired and the best housing is allocated, according to family needs and seniority.

Also, the work on a kibbutz is very physically hard and, although an 8-hour day and a 6-day week are the norm, very frequently members are required to work additional hours, especially at harvest-time. To hire outside labour goes completely against the kibbutz ideal, but is happening more and more often. Holidays are sometimes a problem too. Everyone feels the need to get away from their everyday work and the kibbutzim have tried to cater for this by buying homes in different parts of the country for their members to use. Nowadays they often pay for trips abroad for their members. The early kibbutzim operated a system of work mobility, which means moving from job to job, to make work more interesting. Today, however, this could make the kibbutz economically inefficient. There needs to be a careful balance between running a successful business and satisfying the needs of the members.

The position of women is something which has always posed problems. One of the original aims of the kibbutzim was to free the women from household tasks and give them complete equality with men. What has happened, however, is that some women have found themselves working in the kitchens, laundries and children's houses and so, instead of being freed from these tasks, they have become burdened even more by doing these jobs full-time for years on end. Some women do work in agriculture and industry on the kibbutzim, but certainly the original hopes and ambitions have not yet been fully realized.

The kibbutz has seen many changes over the years and possibly one of the greatest has been the huge improvement in the standard of living. The first pioneers led a very primitive existence, but today's kibbutzniks — at any rate on the older and richer kibbutzim — have swimming pools and many other sporting and cultural facilities. Orchestras, choirs, art, poetry, drama, folk singing, dancing, hiking, table tennis, chess and films are popular kibbutz activities. Many kibbutzim have their own untraditional ways of celebrating Jewish festivals, with strong emphasis on their agricultural and national features and (often) very little religious content. They have also instituted some new festivals, such as a sheep-shearing festival to celebrate the end of shearing, and have tried to revive a Festival of the Vineyards, which was celebrated in ancient times on the fifteenth of Av but had died out.

Life on a kibbutz is not limited to Israelis, as anyone can experience this unusual way of living. Every year many thousands of young people from all corners of the world come to live and work on a kibbutz for a few weeks or months. The visitor puts in 8 hours of work a day and receives, in exchange, his board and lodging, some trips around Israel, but, most of all, an insight into a completely different way of life.

The Youth Movement

There are many different youth organizations in Israel and their total membership of both Jewish and non-Jewish boys and girls exceeds 250,000. The largest group — Ha-No'ar Ha'oved Ve-Halomed ("Working and Learning Youth") — was founded in 1924 and has over 100,000 members. This organization is closely related to the kibbutz movement and to the Histadrut (the Labour Federation). The second largest is Hatzofim ("The Scouts"), which was founded in 1919 and is affiliated to the International Scout Movement. About 40,000 young people belong to this group, including 15,000 Arabs.

Caring for People

Like many countries Israel has a National Insurance Scheme which provides financial help for the sick, handicapped, unemployed, poor and elderly. There is also a comprehensive Mother and Child Care Service. This has 800 units, including 75 in Arab towns and villages. There are 80 hospitals and specialized clinics in Israel. Especially famous is the Hadassah-Hebrew University Medical Centre in Jerusalem.

Stamps to commemorate the Magen David Adom Jubilee.

Magen David Adom

In 1930 a First Aid Society was established in Tel Aviv. It was called Magen David Adom (M.D.A.) — Red Shield of David. Today, the M.D.A. is a parallel body to the Red Cross found in other countries. It provides the same services as the Red Cross — for example, an ambulance service, blood donor service and first aid courses. Unfortunately, in modern Israel's short history there have been many wars and outbursts of terrorism. A further function of M.D.A., therefore, is to serve the armed forces — in fact, it was founded originally as the medical wing of the Haganah (page 24).

By 1948 malaria had been successfully wiped out and the general level of health improved. Mass immigration, however, brought with it a series of new health problems, and the M.D.A. found itself busier than ever. Its educational role became especially important as many of the immigrants from eastern countries had little knowledge of hygiene.

M.D.A. is predominantly a voluntary organization. It has about 5,000 members working around a central core of paid professionals. The importance of possessing some knowledge of first aid is greatly emphasized and each year more than 35,000 Israelis participate in the M.D.A. basic first aid course. In 1974 an M.D.A. youth group (15-18 year olds) was established. This now has 1,800 young volunteers.

Like the Red Cross, M.D.A. sends aid to other countries affected by natural disasters or war. Moreover, as Israel has faced and conquered many health problems common to developing lands, students from Third World countries often come to study here.

September

Greeting the New Year

September marks the beginning of a season of festivals in Israel. These commence with Rosh Hashanah, the Jewish New Year, a two-day holiday falling on the first and second of Tishri. It may seem odd that the New Year comes at the beginning of the seventh month rather than the first (page 6), and a possible explanation is that in older times the Jews did indeed regard the year as starting in the autumn, when the harvest had been gathered in and the agricultural year completed. Later, they adopted the Babylonian custom of counting the months from Nisan, in the spring. Nevertheless, they continued to regard the beginning of Tishri as the New Year for many purposes: for instance, the chronological year starts then. The Jewish year 5744 began in September 1983, on the first of Tishri.

The New Year is a solemn festival, for it is regarded as the day on which God judges mankind and determines the fate of each individual for the coming year. An important part of the synagogue service is the blowing of a ram's horn, called "shofar" in Hebrew. This is a very ancient custom, for which many explanations were later offered. A popular one is that the ram's horn is to remind Jewish people of God's love and

Two different styles of Jewish New Year card. The second is a painting of Moses receiving the Tablets of the Law, by Shalom of Safed, b. 1887.

mercy as they recall the story of Abraham and Isaac. As a test of Abraham's faith, God ordered him to sacrifice his only son, Isaac. Just as Abraham was about to kill Isaac, who lay bound on the altar, an angel stopped him and told him to set his son free: "And Abraham lifted up his eyes and looked, and behold, behind him was a ram, caught in a thicket by his horns; and Abraham went and took the ram and offered it up as a burnt offering instead of his son." (Genesis 22:13).

The Day of Atonement

The Day of Atonement, Yom Kippur, is the holiest day of the Jewish year, the culmination of the "ten days of Penitence" which commence with Rosh Hashanah. During these ten days people are supposed to reflect on their life and behaviour during the past year. On Yom Kippur, everything in Israel stops: restaurants and shops are closed (except in Arab areas), and there are no radio or television broadcasts. Yom Kippur itself is a day of fasting. People deny themselves all food and water from sunset to sunset and spend the day in the synagogue, praying and repenting, asking God to forgive the sins they have committed during the past year. Yom Kippur is the penitent's last

chance to alter the fate determined for him or her on Rosh Hashanah. The service ends with a long continuous blast on the shofar, and everyone goes home to break the fast.

In School

The beginning of September sees the start of a new school year. Education has a special task to perform in Israel, that of welding together children whose parents came from many different countries and cultures. Immigrants arrive in Israel with an enormous variety of educational experience and ability, ranging from total illiteracy to university standard.

Nursery, primary and secondary education is free, but further education has to be paid for. Parents can choose to send their children to either state schools, state religious schools or very orthodox religious schools. The majority choose the first.

Hebrew is the first language in Jewish schools, with Arabic second; the reverse is true in Arab schools. Arab Israelis have benefited greatly under Israel's school system, and attendance and attainment have risen dramatically in the last thirty years. In traditional Muslim culture it was not considered important for a woman to be

---

HONEY CAKE

A Traditional Cake for Rosh Hashanah

½ lb/250 grammes Honey
2 eggs
½ teaspoon Bicarbonate
¼ pint/5 fl. oz warm water
shredded almonds

4 oz/125 grammes Caster Sugar
½ teaspoon mixed spice
12 oz/375 grammes S R Flour
1 teaspoon ground ginger
3 tablespoons cooking oil

Sieve the flour, ginger, spice and bicarbonate. Warm the honey. Beat eggs and sugar till frothy, add oil and honey, then dry ingredients alternately with the water. Mix to a smooth batter. Turn into shallow greased tin approximately 9"/22 cm diameter. Sprinkle with shredded almonds and bake for about 1 hour. Mark 4/375°F.

---

educated, but as it is compulsory under Israeli law for girls to attend school, Arab women in Israel are comparatively well-educated. There is now often great pride in the Arab villages when their girls return, often as teachers and nurses. There are at present about 2,000 Arab students studying in Higher Education.

Israeli children learn all the usual subjects, but of particular interest is the history of their country, much of it being learnt by studying the Bible. Israeli schoolchildren are very fond of hiking round the countryside studying the landscape and the flowers.

Most Israelis do not go on to higher education until after their army service. This means that Israeli students are older than British students and often they are married and have families to support as well as fees to pay. Many students therefore have a job as well as studying. Nevertheless, Israeli universities have managed to maintain very high standards.

An Ancient Language Revived

Among the members of the First Aliyah (page 8) there were many who believed that the Jews returning to their ancient homeland should begin to speak Hebrew, as the ancient Jews had done. Many Jews still knew Hebrew, although they did not normally speak it (just as many people in Europe knew Latin well, although no-one used it as his everyday language). They decided to try to make Hebrew the language of the schools they set up in their small, isolated villages. This did not just mean that the teachers taught the children Hebrew as though it were a foreign language, but that they actually spoke in Hebrew all the time, whatever subject they were teaching, and even in ordinary conversations outside the classroom. They also encouraged the children to speak Hebrew to one another. The first school to do this was in the village of Rishon le-Zion ("First in Zion") in 1888. Ten years later the first Hebrew-speaking kindergarten was opened in the same village.

Between about 1900 and 1910 young men and women who had been through the Hebrew school system of these villages, and who spoke Hebrew naturally, began to get married, and their children grew up in homes where they heard no other language, so that they acquired Hebrew as their mother-tongue. Hebrew was a fully-alive language again for the first time for 1,700 years. Today, it is the first language of the majority of Israelis. There are centres where adult immigrants can go for crash courses to teach them Hebrew as quickly as possible so that they can get out and about and feel at home. The name for such a centre is "ulpan". The mass immigration in the early years of state-hood forced the Israelis to do a great deal of research into ways of teaching people Hebrew quickly, and through the ulpanim they have become very successful.

Hebrew is very different from English. It belongs to the Semitic family of languages, which also includes Arabic, whereas English, like French and German, is an Indo-European language. Hebrew is written in a different alphabet and is written from right to left. One reason for this is that, originally, the letters were chiselled in stone, not written on paper, and the craftsmen would have held their chisel in their left hand and hammer in the right; consequently, it was easier to work from right to left than from left to right.

When people try to write Hebrew words using the English alphabet, it is often impossible to find exact sound-equivalents. This explains why one Hebrew word may be written in more than one way in English. For example, Hanukkah — the name of a Jewish festival (page 63) — may also be written Chanukka. The Hebrew word begins with a letter which is pronounced rather like the "ch" in the Scottish "loch". Similarly, the town-name Eilat is sometimes written Elath.

In spite of the difference between the languages, a few English words are derived

SOME HEBREW WORDS

English	Sound	Hebrew
Peace	Sha-lom	שלום
Good Morning	Bo-ker Tov	בקר טוב
Good Evening	E-rev Tov	ערב טוב
How are you	Ma Shlom-kha	מה שלומך
Please	B'va-ka-sha	בבקשה
Thank you	To-da	תודה
Pardon	Sli-ha	סליחה
Yes	Ken	כן
No	Lo	לא
Maybe	Oo-lie (rhymes with "guys")	אולי
Good	Tov	טוב
Bad	Ra	רע
Man	Ish	איש
Woman	Isha	אשה
Boy	Ye-led	ילד
Girl	Yal-da	ילדה

from older Hebrew ones. Examples are Amen, Hallelujah, Jubilee, and Sabbath. Many English names, too, come from Hebrew names in the Bible: David, John, James, Simon, Anne, Mary, and Elizabeth are examples.

The second language of Israel is Arabic, and in most areas signs are written in both Hebrew and Arabic. For people who do not know either alphabet, they are often also written in the Latin alphabet (the one used for English and most European languages).

Farming

Among the first Zionist settlers who arrived in Palestine at the turn of the century, there was a strong wish to "return to the land". In many countries, Jews had not been allowed to own land or to farm it (in fact, many occupations had been forbidden them) and they had tended to become town-dwellers. Antisemites used to claim that Jews were all middlemen, making their livings by trading in commodities which they did little to produce; the Zionists were determined that in Palestine this should not be said of them.

The members of the Second Aliyah, in particular, put great importance on the value of physical labour and working with their own hands, rather than hiring Arab workers. The first hurdle was to buy land. Once bought, it often needed a lot of work to make it fit for agriculture. Developing unpromising lands such as the northern swamps and the southern deserts has always been one of the remarkable features of Israeli farming.

Some areas were farmed for reasons of national security. The Israeli government felt that putting settlements close to the borders, or in nearly-empty parts of the country, would help in the defence of the State and in establishing a clear-cut claim to disputed lands. Other sites were farmed simply because of the good farm land they offered.

The arable farms produce many industrial crops such as cotton, groundnuts and sugar beet. It has taken many years of experimenting to find which crops are most suited to the climate and soil. An increasing number of sheep are grazed and bred, mainly for

Jaffa is a familiar name to all fruit lovers and is synonymous with large, sweet juicy oranges and grapefruit. This marketing name was taken from the ancient port of Jaffa (see page 59).

At the end of the nineteenth century, some of the first Zionist immigrants settled in Jaffa and the population grew. Increasing numbers led many families to make their homes slightly north of Jaffa, and they called their settlement Tel Aviv (Hill of Spring). In the 1920s and 1930s Tel Aviv expanded rapidly, and suburbs around Tel Aviv began to grow. Some of these have interesting names:

Ramat Gan — "Garden Heights" (The Diamond Centre and Tel Aviv University)
Petach Tikva — "Gateway to Hope" (The earliest of the pioneering farming villages, founded in 1878, but now a suburb of Tel Aviv)
Bat Yam — "Daughter of Sea"

Today, Tel Aviv has easily outgrown Jaffa, and the population of the Tel Aviv metropolis is well over a million. It is accepted as the centre of modern Israel, looking towards the future rather than the past. It has a very different atmosphere to Jerusalem, especially at night, when it becomes the nerve centre for vibrant night life in Israel. The cafes on and around Dizengoff Street are alive with Israelis and tourists, young and old. The air is filled with chatter and laughter and there is a constant buzz of excitement throughout the city.

Aerial view of Tel Aviv.

Jaffa oranges ready for export at Haifa docks.

their milk, most of which becomes cheese. Farmers are experimenting with different breeds of livestock, and Israel has many productive fish farms, mainly producing carp, which provides a cheap source of protein. Turkeys and chickens are reared in vast numbers for their meat and eggs, but Israel is probably known best of all for its fruit and vegetables. Jaffa oranges and grapefruit, melons, cucumbers, aubergines, grapes and olives are all native to Israel, while apples, bananas, plums, avocados, lettuce, chinese leaves, beans, peas and asparagus are varieties which have all been successfully introduced.

While most Jewish farmers work either on a kibbutz or on a moshav, those Arabs in

Israel who are engaged in agriculture are either independent farmers or farm labourers. Much of the Arab farmland is around Lake Kinneret and in other parts of Galilee. The main crops are grains, tobacco, fruit, vegetables and olives.

The Moshav — An Alternative to the Kibbutz

The moshav is a co-operative agricultural village and is a cross between a kibbutz and an independent farm. Not everyone wanted such a high degree of communal living as there is on a kibbutz (page 42); yet people realized that much can be gained by sharing some facilities, and so the idea of a moshav was born. The first moshav settlement was established in 1921 in the Jezreel Valley, and was called Nahalal. There are two types of moshav, the moshav shitufi and the moshav ovdim; the majority of moshav members belong to the latter.

On a moshav ovdim ("workers' settlement") the land is divided into smallholdings, each run by one family which lives in its own house. The cooperative element comes in because the moshav as a whole buys and maintains the more expensive kinds of equipment, markets its members' produce, and builds such things as the central irrigation network, dairy, and refrigeration plant. The moshav shitufi ("collective moshav") has features of both the moshav ovdim and the kibbutz. Production is on a collective basis, as on a kibbutz; the land is not divided into smallholdings but farmed collectively. However, each family has its own home and is responsible for its domestic economy and the care of its children, as on a moshav

ovdim. A moshav shitufi may also include some light industry in addition to farming.

The moshav movement expanded rapidly in the 1950s when many immigrants arrived in a short time. Most of these immigrants were very different in background and outlook from the Russian-Jewish immigrants of fifty years previously, who had founded the kibbutz movement. The immigrants of the fifties came mainly from Arab countries such as Yemen and Morocco and had never been influenced by the socialist ideas which were so widespread in Russia. These immigrants were not attracted to life on a kibbutz, but adapted well to moshav existence.

Initially, immigrants from one country did not really want to mix with immigrants from another. They wanted the security of their own language, foods, customs and culture around them. To try to meet both the needs of the immigrants and the needs of the country, the government set up co-operative villages, built round a central town. In each village, the families had the same cultural background and so felt reasonably

A moshav in the Jezreel Valley.

secure. They used the town for marketing their produce, for high schools, factories, hospitals and theatres. In this way, the immigrants slowly became acclimatized to their new country and gradually got used to mixing with other immigrants and sabras as they met in the urban centre.

A good example of this system working is the Lachish region in the Negev. There are 29 villages based around the town of Kiryat Gat, which was founded in 1955. Kiryat Gat processes the cotton and sugar beet grown by the farmers and provides all the economic and social services that the villagers need. This experiment has proved to be so successful that many Third World developing countries are adopting the same system as a way of improving their agricultural efficiency. Many young members of the moshav movement go abroad to help establish moshavim in African, Asian and South American countries.

October

In the orthodox section of Jerusalem, each family builds its own sukkah.

Rejoicing – Sukkot

The autumn festivities continue into October, with a change of mood from solemn to joyous. The festival of Sukkot (i.e., Booths. The word rhymes with "Book lot") recalls the forty years when the Children of Israel were wandering in the desert with their leader Moses. A sukkah is a simple open-roofed building commemorating those in which the Children of Israel would have lived, and each synagogue and most individual homes have their own sukkah.

The sukkot are very simply built, since they are only up for eight days each year. They are usually erected against one of the walls of the house, which thus also serves as a wall of the sukkah. The other walls can be made in various ways — for instance, by nailing boards together. The roof is mainly branches and leaves, through which the sky and stars are visible. White sheets are hung inside the sukkah against the walls, and the sukkah is decorated with fruit and flowers. Flat-dwellers in Israel build sukkot on their balconies. It is the custom to eat all meals in the sukkah and orthodox Jews usually sleep in it, too, in obedience to the biblical commandment "You shall dwell in booths . . . that your generations may know that I made the people of Israel dwell in booths when I brought them out of the Land of Egypt" (Leviticus 23:42-43).

As well as commemorating the years of wandering in the wilderness, Sukkot is also the last of the three great agricultural festivals. In earlier times it celebrated the ingathering from the threshing-floor and the wine press.

More Rejoicing – Simhat Torah

Simhat Torah — Rejoicing in the Torah — is the day on which the annual reading of the Torah is completed and immediately begun again. Every synagogue has an "ark", a compartment like a cupboard with decorated curtains in front of the doors. This contains one or more parchment scrolls, usually about a metre high, wound onto wooden poles with handles at each end. The scroll contains the text of the entire Torah, or Pentateuch — the Five Books of Moses — and it is brought out during the weekly

Eating a meal in a sukkah.

Sabbath service so that a section of the Torah can be read out loud from it, using a traditional form of chant. It takes a year to get through the whole work, beginning and ending on Simhat Torah. As the last of the

Celebrating Simhat Torah in Tel Aviv.

LINKS WITH THE PAST

Time	People	What happened	Links with Today
17th century BCE	Abraham and Sarah	Abraham receives divine call and promise of nationhood. Goes to the land of Canaan.	All Patriarchs (Abraham, Isaac and Jacob, the forefathers of the Jews) and wives (except Rachel) buried in the Cave of Machpelah outside Hebron.
	Isaac		
	Jacob Joseph	Migration to Egypt. Enslavement.	
13th century BCE	Moses	Exodus from Egypt.	Festival of Passover. Ten Commandments. Shavuot. Sukkot. Jebel Musa — a possible site of the biblical Mt Sinai.
	Joshua	Conquest of Canaan.	
12th and 11th centuries BCE	Judges	Consolidation of Israelites' hold on Canaan.	Song of Deborah (Judges, ch. 5).
	King Saul	Establishment of monarchy.	
c. 1000 BCE	David	David fights and beats Goliath. Becomes King. Makes Jerusalem his capital.	Book of Psalms (attributed to David). Supposed tomb of David in Jerusalem.
965-928 BCE	King Solomon	Solomon builds Temple.	Song of Songs, Book of Proverbs, Ecclesiastes (all attributed to Solomon).
928 BCE		Division into two kingdoms, Judah (south) and Israel (north).	
586 BCE		Destruction of Temple. Mass deportation to Babylonia.	Many archaeological remains in Jerusalem.
538-515 BCE	Cyrus, King of Persia	Cyrus allows Jews to return to Holy Land. Second Temple built.	
164 BCE	Judah Maccabee	Judah Maccabee captures Jerusalem; rededicates the Temple.	Hanukkah.
37-4 BCE	King Herod	Herod rebuilds and enlarges the Temple. Constructs or renovates many other buildings.	Fortresses of Herodium and Masada. Aqueduct to serve Caesarea. Theatre at Caesarea. Western Wall of the Temple Mount.
1 BCE-30 CE (approx.)	Jesus	Jesus attracts many followers by his preaching and his power of healing. He is crucified by the Romans.	Christmas. Easter. Church of the Holy Sepulchre.
132-135 CE	Simeon Bar Kokhba	Further rebellion against Rome.	Bar Kokhba letters.

five "books", Deuteronomy, is finished, so the first one, Genesis, is started. The idea is of a circle, or unity — there is no beginning and no end, simply a continuous recitation of the Holy Law.

On Simhat Torah the Scrolls are carried in procession round the synagogue and often into the streets. Children following the procession carry flags adorned with apples, in which burning candles are fixed. A good deal of dancing and revelry takes place, in the synagogue as well as at home and outside.

Links from Past to Present

Archaeology is said to be the Israelis' second most favourite activity, the first being talking! The foundations for new buildings are laid with vigilant eyes, in case anything important is dug up. Farmers are also constantly on the look-out for ancient remains as they plough new ground. Archaeology can show us how people in the past lived, and this knowledge can, surprisingly, often help us solve problems today. Avdat is an ancient ruined city in the middle of the desert, 40 miles south of Beersheba. The original citizens provided shelter and food for desert travellers and found ways of tapping the underground water supplies. Avdat was built during the second century BCE and abandoned in the tenth century CE, but the remains show us how the inhabitants irrigated their land and modern scientists look carefully to see if their ancient methods can be adapted for today's desert farmers.

Material links between the past and the present go back many thousands of years. In Hebron is the Cave of Machpelah where the Patriarchs, the family of Abraham, are buried. Jews lived in that area until 1929, when many were massacred by Arab rioters and the rest fled, not to return until 1967, when Hebron was captured by the Israelis in the Six-Day War. Ancient copper mines, said to be King Solomon's Mines, have been located in the Negev, and modern open-pit mines have been producing copper there since

Solomon's Pillars at Timna in the Negev Desert.

ACRE

Acre is a very old sea port and was used as a fortress by the Crusaders, whose capital it was for a time. More recently, during the British Mandate, the Jewish Underground Movement organized a spectacular prison break from the top-security prison there. Today, visitors can walk round the prison and gaze in horror at the execution cell where hangings took place, and at the initials of past prisoners carved in the walls. The old walled town has a traditional Arab quarter and houses the imposing Mosque of al-Jazzar. Acre is predominantly an Arab town and has a population of 36,000.

ASHDOD

Once an important Philistine city which declined under Roman rule and eventually disappeared, Ashdod was resurrected by the Israelis to relieve the pressure on Haifa and is Israel's newest port. A new deep-water harbour was built and provides port facilities purely for freight goods. Raw materials from abroad pass through Ashdod en route to factories in the south of Israel, and the finished goods travel in the reverse direction. Ancient Ashdod was three miles (4½ km) from the Mediterranean coast. The modern city is on the seashore.

TIBERIAS

Tiberias is a town on the Western shore of Lake Kinneret (the Sea of Galilee). It has a very hot climate and is a popular holiday resort. The hot springs there are beneficial for sufferers from rheumatic ailments, and for the more energetic there is water skiing, swimming or boat trips on the lake.

Tiberias was founded by Herod Antipas, son of King Herod, and named after the Roman emperor Tiberius, who was then on the throne. The city walls were built by the crusaders. Tiberias was the main Jewish centre in Palestine from the end of the second century CE until the Arab conquest in the seventh century, when the Jewish religious authorities moved to Jerusalem.

Across the lake from Tiberias is Kibbutz Ein Gev, where music and folklore festivals are held in the spring and autumn. North of Tiberias lies the ancient town of Safed which has been an important Jewish centre since the fifteenth century when Jewish refugees from Spain settled there. Today there is a thriving artists' colony in Safed and they mix together ancient traditions with modern designs.

Masada, showing the Roman encampments and the ramp they built, by which they eventually stormed the fortress.

1959. From excavations and documents, we know that Ashdod and Acre were previously busy ports. The Roman theatre at Caesarea has been restored and is now used for concerts. The city from which Jonah set sail on the voyage which led to his being swallowed by a big fish was Jaffa. From clothing remains found in caves, we know that early Jews living near Kiryat Gat were competent weavers, and today the same town houses textile firms. It is interesting that, during the time of the Second Temple, about half a million people lived around Lake Kinneret and the hot springs round Tiberias made the town a popular resort even then.

Masada is one of the most extensively excavated sites in Israel. This great fortress rising majestically out of the desert and over-looking the Dead Sea reminds Israelis of the courageous last stand of their ancestors against the Romans. In 72 CE Jerusalem and the Temple had been destroyed, but more than 900 Zealots continued to resist the might of the Roman Empire. After a pro-longed siege, the Romans built an enormous ramp and succeeded in breaching the walls of the fortress. The Zealots knew this was the end, but, rather than become slaves of the Romans, ten men were chosen to put to death the rest of the people, and one of the ten was chosen to slay the other nine. This last man finally took his own life, after making sure that all their possessions were destroyed, except for food, so that the Romans would see that death had been voluntary, not through lack of food. Not all died, however: two women and five children hid and were spared by the Romans and it is through their retelling of the story as related by the historian Josephus, that we know what happened. Today, many Israelis and visitors go to Masada, and begin the walk up the steep, rocky Snake Path at about three o'clock in the morning, guided only by moonlight and torchlight. They arrive at the top in time to watch the sun rise over Jordan and the Dead Sea, a most spectacular event as the sky is slowly washed with crimson glows. For the less energetic there is now-adays a cable car.

Jerusalem has many reminders of the past. Outside the Knesset stands a large, seven-branched Menorah (candelabrum) presented by British Members of Parliament. The seven-branched candelabrum was a prominent feature of the portable sanctuary constructed by the Children of Israel in the wilderness after the Exodus from Egypt, and, later, of the Jerusalem Temple. The Arch of Titus, in Rome, clearly shows it being carried away as part of the Roman spoils of 70 CE. It came to be regarded as a symbol of the Jews and of their religion and has been found on grave-stones, mosaics, synagogues and coins. It is now the official emblem of the State of Israel.

Sport

The two most popular outdoor sports in Israel are soccer and basketball. These are followed by swimming, tennis, handball, volleyball, fencing and yachting. If little is heard in Britain about Israeli sporting activities, this is because Israel belongs to the Asian Games Federation, except for basket-ball and volleyball, where the country com-petes in the European zone.

A non-competitive form of sport that is very popular in Israel is marching. The main event is an annual four-day march to Jerusalem, organized by the Israel Defence Forces. Thousands of people of all ages take part, organized in groups — families, clubs, factories, and so on. They go out onto the hills around Jerusalem, marching together with groups of soldiers in training. The Army builds camps and lays on entertain-ments. The event culminates in a march through the streets of Jerusalem. There are also many one-day marches in other parts of the country. Also popular, and open to all, is the swim across Lake Kinneret every year.

Every four years the Maccabiah takes place in Israel. This is a kind of Jewish

Olympics (it is recognized by the International Olympic Committee). It is organized by the Maccabi World Union, a Jewish sports organization named after Judah Maccabee (page 63), and the first one took place in 1932. The Maccabiah draws together Jewish athletes from all over the world, to compete in every sport.

Less physically tiring, but still very demanding is the International Chess competition held bi-annually in Israel. Both chess and bridge are very popular pastimes among all age groups.

The annual four-day march to Jerusalem.

November

Economy and Industry

At the beginning of 1948, on the eve of independence, the Jewish economy in Palestine was in a precarious state. Only a small part of the better agricultural land was owned by the J.N.F., much potentially-fertile swamp had still to be drained, and there was little industry. When the State of Israel came into existence, on 14 May, it immediately had to finance a war against its Arab neighbours. Even when the war ended, in 1949, the Arab countries which, from the economic and geographical point of view, were Israel's natural trading partners, refused to trade with it and did their best to stop other countries from doing so. With the departure of the British, Israel also ceased to be part of the sterling area. Into this economic catastrophe arrived thousands of

---

EILAT

Eilat, on the Red Sea, has a split personality. On the one hand it is a thriving tourist resort with visitors taking advantage of its very clear water to go skin-diving. There is beautiful coral to admire and exotic tropical fish to wonder at. For the less energetic there are boats with glass bottoms to look through and underwater observation units.

The other Eilat is a busy port which provides Israel with an outlet, via the Red Sea, to the Persian Gulf and the Far East.

---

immigrants . . . all welcome, but all requiring food, clothes, training, jobs and roofs over their heads. A further problem was finding the finance for defence, a major concern at the time.

Initial financial aid came to Israel from the Diaspora. In 1948 the Diaspora con-

EMPLOYMENT

Areas of Employment	Number Employed (1980)	Percentage of Population
Public and Community Services	370,000	30%
Industry	280,000	23%
Commerce	150,000	12%
Construction	120,000	10%
Agriculture	70,000	6%
Transport and Communications	80,000	6%
Finance and Business	76,000	6%
Personal and Other	68,000	6%
Electricity and Water	10,000	1%

tributed 33% of Israel's revenue — by 1960 this had diminished to 8%. Three main explanations for this were loans from America and other countries; money received as Reparations and Restitution from Germany (this was money paid by Germany to compensate Israel for the cost of rehabilitating Jews who had settled there after escaping or surviving Nazi persecution during the Second World War, and paid to individual Jews — many of whom lived in Israel — whose relations had been murdered or whose health or careers had been damaged by the Nazis); and the increasing discovery and exploitation of natural resources, which meant that the economy could expand from within rather than through external financial aid. The land itself was a major resource as many industries are based on agricultural produce. The Bible mentions the presence of bitumen in the Dead Sea area (Genesis 14: 10) and indeed supplies of chemicals such as sulphur, potash, and bromide were discovered there. In the north, glass, stone, marble, sand and other building materials were found while further research uncovered metal resources. Modern copper mines were opened in 1959 at Timna, near Eilat, close to the site of the ancient workings known as King Solomon's Mines. Last but certainly not least, precious oil was found near Ashkelon.

As these natural resources were developed, the economy began to grow and was soon in a better position to absorb the new immigrants. They could find work on the farms or in the new factories. In turn, the population growth aided industrial growth, for there were more people requiring goods. The early 1960s were boom years. Unemployment was unheard-of and, once able to meet its own needs, the country began to increase its exports. Economic growth continued after the Six-Day War, but in 1974 the economy was badly hit by the increased oil prices. Israel, like many other countries, found itself suffering rising prices and inflation.

CURRENCY

In 1980 the Israeli legal tender was changed from the Lira to the Shekel (IS). This is divided into 100 agorot.

Israeli Money	English Value (May 1983)
Coins 1 agora	less
5 agorot	than
10 agorot	1p
50 agorot (½ shekel)	
Notes IS 1	1.56p
IS 5	7.81p
IS 10	15.63p
IS 50	78.12p
IS 100	£1.56p

Haifa is said to be one of the most beautiful cities in the world. From the top of Mount Carmel there are magnificent views of Haifa Bay and the golden-domed Baha'i Temple, which is surrounded by exotic Persian Gardens which cling to the steep mountainside.

The deep water bay made Haifa a natural choice for a port and it was completed in 1934. As well as passenger lines, the Merchant Fleet of the Navy is now based there.

A unique feature of this busy city is the Carmelit, an underground railway, stretching over a mile and climbing 275 metres from the Port to the top of Mount Carmel. It has only two trains, pulled by cable. One train starts from the top at exactly the same time as the other starts from the bottom and they pass each other half-way, at the only section of the tunnel wide enough. The distances between stations match exactly, since both trains have to stop at the same time.

Today three-quarters of Israel's income comes from the export of ten major commodity groups. Polished diamonds and citrus fruits head the list, followed by chemical and oil products, clothing, fertilizers, fruit and vegetables, metal products, textiles, food products and electrical and electronic equipment.

A Sparkling Business

The diamond industry began in Israel in 1937, in a small cow shed in Petach Tikvah. Today, diamonds are Israel's largest export and the country is second only to Belgium among the world's leading diamond centres. This phenomenal growth was partly due to the fact that during the Second World War many diamond-polishing experts fled from Nazi-occupied Belgium and Holland to the relative safety of Israel, taking their skills with them. (In fact, Palestine replaced these two countries as the gem-diamond centre of the free world for the duration of the war.) The jewel industry in Israel is expanding further, and now emeralds are also being cut and polished, for the country possesses cutting and polishing techniques that are among the most sophisticated in the world.

Tourism

Tourism is one of Israel's oldest trades, as religious pilgrims have been making visits to the Holy Land for many centuries. Today, tourists come not only to see the religious shrines and holy cities, but also to enjoy the Mediterranean climate and exciting desert scenery. Eilat is on the Red Sea and is almost always hot (it is Israel's southern most point). Tiberias and the Dead Sea are in the rift valley which is below sea-level and are also pretty warm in winter. Israel is well-endowed with health resorts which have developed from the natural spring waters. Young people are attracted to the kibbutz life-style and also the archaeological digs, both being unusual ways to spend a summer vacation. In 1978, 1,176,000 tourists visited the country, compared with 437,000 in 1970, making tourism very much of a growth industry.

Tourists on the beach at Tel Aviv.

62

The Histadrut

The Histadrut (the General Federation of Labour) is Israel's large and powerful trades union organization. It has approximately 2,360,000 members. It differs from a British union, because it is also one of the country's largest employers, employing 20% of the labour force. Such is the influence of the Histadrut that its headquarters in Tel Aviv used to be nicknamed "the Kremlin", by Israelis who felt that it was too powerful an institution. Like most unions it operates a sick fund, medical care facilities, welfare services, schools, hospitals, social and sporting activities and negotiates wage settlements. Many Israeli salaries are linked to a consumer Price Index, which means that, as the cost of living rises, so do the wages.

December

The Miracle of Hanukkah

The year draws to a close with a busy and joyful month for both Jewish and Christian Israelis. Jews all over the world as well as in Israel celebrate the festival of Lights, Hanukkah. This recalls the successful revolt against the King of Syria — led by Judah Maccabee, culminating in the entry of his victorious

An unusual menorah with Jaffa oranges as candle holders.

◁ *Performing a play for Hanukkah.*

63

army into Jerusalem in 164 BCE. According to legend, they found that the Syrians had defiled nearly all the oil stored there. There was only one small flask bearing the seal of the High Priest, containing enough oil to keep the Temple menorah (page 59) alight for one day — too little time for a fresh supply to be brought. However, the oil miraculously lasted for eight days. In Jewish homes this miracle is remembered by lighting one candle on an eight-branched menorah on the first night, two candles on the second and so on until there are eight candles shining.

The Holy Land

The State of Israel occupies most of the strip of land between the eastern shore of the Mediterranean Sea and the River Jordan. What gives this tiny area its special importance to mankind is its close associations with three world religions. For Jews and Christians it is the Holy Land — the land promised by God to the Israelite tribes. The birth, ministry, and death of Jesus all took place there. For Muslims, the Temple Mount is the spot from which Mohammed ascended to heaven and this is the third holiest shrine in Islam, preceded only by the building in Mecca called the Ka'aba, and the Mosque of Mohammed in Medina.

Since the Six-Day War in June 1967, some of the main holy places of Christianity and Islam have been under Jewish rule and the Israelis' commitment to "safeguard the Holy Places of all Religions" — set out in their Declaration of Independence of 1948 — has been put to the test. The problem is made very hard by the fact that one site may be holy to two religions. The area of the Temple, in Jerusalem, and the cave of Machpelah, in Hebron, are holy to both Islam and Judaism. Both have been sources of friction in the past and could all too easily be so again.

Judaism

The Jewish religion is the oldest faith in Israel. There are now over three million Jews in Israel, but this makes Israel only the third largest Jewish community in the world. There are more Jews both in America and in Russia. However, Israel is the only country in the world where Jews are a majority and where Judaism is the predominant religion.

The Jewish place of worship is a synagogue and there are over 7,000 synagogues in Israel. Most synagogues are open for services every morning and evening, not just on the Sabbath — though the services on that day are much longer than on weekdays.

There are about 450 officially-appointed rabbis in Israel. A rabbi is a man who has studied Jewish law and the Jewish religion and is qualified to pronounce on religious questions. Rabbis in Israel (unlike those in the Diaspora) do not, for the most part, act as ministers to congregations. The more senior rabbis are judges, sitting in courts, and those lower down the scale are religious functionaries whose duties include, for example, supervising the arrangements for kashrut (page 19) in food shops and hotels in a particular district.

In certain matters, Jewish religious law is recognized as the law of the State, and rabbis who act as judges are classified as civil judges. This applies to marriage and divorce, for instance, and Jews can only be married

POPULATION BY COMMUNITIES					
	Jews	Muslim	Christian	Druze	Total	% of Jews
1949	1,014,000	111,000	34,000	15,000	1,174,000	86.3
1978	3,076,000	444,000	86,000	45,000	3,651,000	84.2

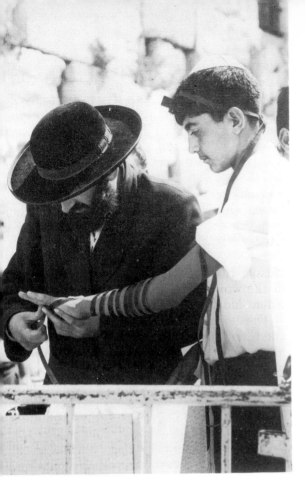

A Jewish boy putting on the phylacteries — small leather boxes containing Hebrew texts.

kept by Jews as the Sabbath, on which they are not allowed to do any work.

In Israel Jewish shops shut on the Sabbath and public transport stops. The Sabbath is very important in Judaism and work finishes early on Friday to allow people time to get home and prepare for it.

The main Jewish festivals are national holidays, much as Christmas and Easter are national holidays in Britain. However, less than a quarter of Israeli Jews are strictly orthodox. Others observe only some of the religious traditions, and many are not religious at all. If they want to spend Sabbath on the beach instead of in the synagogue they may do so, but they must travel to the beach by private car or taxi, since the usual bus services do not operate in most areas. The exceptions are Arab areas, since Arab buses run (and Arab shops are open) on Saturdays.

The Torah lays down rules for many aspects of life, and all official institutions, such as the government and army, recognize these laws. The Israel Defence Force provides religious facilities for its soldiers. Each Army unit has its own synagogue; only kosher food is served; and even submarines have their own Torah scrolls.

Jewish Pilgrims

In the days when the Temple still stood, the festivals of Passover, Shavuot and Sukkot were "pilgrim festivals", when as many people as could came to the Temple from all over the country. In modern times the tradition has been continued, and individuals and groups go to the Western Wall in Jerusalem from all over the country, especially at Sukkot. The area in front of the Wall is now a kind of open-air synagogue, where there are regular prayer services. On Jewish festivals up to 250,000 people may come to the Wall.

Another modern form of pilgrimage is the habit of Jews from other countries to go to Israel for Jewish festivals, especially Passover and New Year. While there, they are likely

or divorced in Israel in accordance with Jewish law. There is no civil marriage, so members of other religions must also get married in a religious ceremony of their own denomination.

The Jewish Sabbath starts at sunset on Friday and finishes at sunset on Saturday. In fact, all days in the Jewish calendar go from dusk to dusk, because that is how the days were reckoned in biblical times. In the story of the world's creation in the Book of Genesis, for instance, it says "And there was evening and there was morning, one day . . . . And there was evening and there was morning, a second day," and so on (Genesis 1:5-8). On the seventh day, God rested from the labours of creation, which is why this day is to visit at least one of the main shrines, such as the Western Wall, the Cave of Machpelah, the Tomb of Rachel, or Mount Zion. Yad Vashem is a more modern pilgrims' shrine — a memorial to the six million Jews murdered between 1941 and 1945 by the Nazis. In the Hall of Names, a low-ceilinged, dimly-lit room, an eternal flame burns and the floor is inscribed with the names of the 21 largest death camps to which Jewish men, women and children were taken from all over Europe to be killed. Outside is the Avenue of the Righteous Gentiles, a tree-lined boulevard in honour of those non-Jews who risked their lives to help Jews during the Second World War. The hill on which Yad Vashem stands in named Memorial Hill. The name Yad Vashem means "A Monument and a Name", and is taken from Isaiah 56:5, "I will give in my house and within my walls a monument and a name . . . I will give them an everlasting name which shall not be cut off."

Islam

Five times a day the voice of the muezzin can be heard from the minarets in the Muslim areas, calling faithful Muslims to prayer. The Islamic religion originated between 610 and 632 CE when Mohammed,

a great prophet who was born into an Arab tribe from Mecca, claimed to have had visions in which many great things were revealed to him by the true God Allah.

As the Jews live by the Torah, so the Muslims follow the guidelines and laws of the Holy Koran, the book in which God's revelations to Mohammed are set down. There are about 450,000 Muslim citizens of the State of Israel, 12% of the total population. Islamic holy places in Israel are managed by the Muslim Department of the Ministry of Religious Affairs and the salaries of Muslim religious judges and functionaries are paid by the State. The Arabic station of the Israel Broadcasting Authority broadcasts daily readings from the Koran, as well as prayers and sermons each Friday (the day of communal prayer in Islam) and on Muslim festivals.

Christian Pilgrims

There are 86,000 Christian citizens in Israel and the majority of these are Arabs. This is not really a great number when one considers that the Christian faith was born in Israel with the life, death and resurrection of Jesus. The Christian relationship to the Holy Land is very different from that of the Jews. For the latter, Israel is the home of their nation, in which most of its early history took place. Throughout the country, everywhere one walks, one is standing on different periods of Jewish history; different dramatic, tragic or happy events. The Christians' relationship to the Holy Land, however, is based on the birth, life and death of one man.

In Bethlehem the Church of the Nativity marks the spot where Jesus was born. The entrance to the church is very low and

◁ *Inside the Dome of the Rock. The rock bears a mark which is said to be the footprint of Burac, the mare which carried Mohammed on his "Night Journey".*

66

A street in Nazareth.

The Church of the Nativity in Bethlehem.

legend says that this is so you have to bow your head to enter and so humble yourself. Christian pilgrims flock to the ancient Arab town. They wander to the field where the angel appeared to tell the shepherds of the birth of Jesus. They walk down Milk Grotto

---

NAZARETH

Nazareth is an important Arab town in Galilee, nearly half of whose population are Christians. It contains the largest church in the Middle East — the Church of the Annunciation, which marks the place where the Angel Gabriel appeared to Mary to announce the coming birth of Jesus. There are many churches in Nazareth and the Church of St Joseph is built over the cave which is believed to have been Mary and Joseph's home and his workshop.

Nazareth is a busy, sprawling town with a lively Arab bazaar where the locals and tourists mix to barter and haggle for religious baubles, relics and everyday household items. Although many homes have modern conveniences, the old city, with its donkeys, open stalls in the market, and women drawing water from Mary's Well, gives one a feeling of stepping back in time.

---

where Mary is said to have spilt milk while nursing the baby. At Christmas, the bells ring out from Bethlehem, and Manger Square is overflowing with thousands of pilgrims from all over the world, singing carols and remembering the birth of Christ.

After visiting Nazareth, where Jesus spent much of his early life, the pilgrims proceed to Cana where, the Bible tells us, Jesus performed his first miracle — turning water into wine at a wedding feast. The church in Cana is believed to have been built over the very spot where the miracle occurred. There are 300 chapels and churches in Israel and many of these are built on sites where events of importance to the Christian religion took place. Walking by the Sea of Galilee (now called Lake Kinneret), one remembers how Jesus met the first of his disciples, (Simon) Peter and Andrew and later James and John.

At the base of the Mount of Olives in Jerusalem is the Garden of Gethsemane, where Jesus went to pray on the night of the Last Supper, and was betrayed when his

The Druze

The Druze are a mysterious sect, which
broke away from Islam nearly a thousand
years ago. They do not discuss the laws of
their religion with outsiders, and some of its
doctrines are revealed only to a select group
even within the Druze community. They
only marry other Druze, and do not accept
converts. There are about 40,000 of them in
Israel (roughly a tenth of the world total),
living in eighteen villages in the north of the
country. The Druze are officially recognized
as a separate religious community by Israeli
law and have their own official courts.

The Samaritans

There are only about 450 Samaritans in the
world today. Like the Jews, the Samaritans
pray in a synagogue; indeed, the sect is
believed to be an off-shoot of Judaism which

disciple, Judas led a group of armed men to
the Garden to seize him. The olive trees
there are so old that tradition says they are
the very trees which heard Jesus pray. One
can follow the path taken by Jesus during
the last days of his life. Each Friday the
Franciscan friars, who have a monastery in
Jerusalem, lead pilgrims down the road Jesus
walked from his place of trial to the site of
his crucifixion, upon which spot is built the
Church of the Holy Sepulchre.

Druze pilgrimage to the tomb of Jethro.

arose in and around Samaria, an ancient city about 40 miles north of Jerusalem. The Samaritans have their own version of the Pentateuch, written in a traditional script which is different from that used in modern Hebrew. They believe Moses to be the only true prophet.

The Samaritans' most holy place is Mount Gerizim, near modern Nablus. They built a temple there in ancient times — probably in the time of Nehemiah, in the fifth century BCE — and still sacrifice sheep on the mountain each year on their Passover. Mount Gerizim was in Jordan before 1967, but has been under Israeli rule since the war of that year. There was also a Samaritan community in Israel proper which, since 1954, has been concentrated in Holon, near Tel Aviv.

The Baha'i Faith

The Baha'i faith is named after its founder, Baha' Allah ("The Splendour of God" — his original name was Mirza Husayn Ali), who was born in Persia in 1817. He joined a Muslim mystical movement which he subsequently led and transformed into a universalist ethical religion, Baha'i, which today has adherents in more than 300 countries. Baha' Allah settled in Palestine, and the world centre of the faith today is Haifa, where its golden-domed temple is a prominent landmark.

The Baha'i Shrine and Garden in Haifa.

The Karaites

The Karaites are a Jewish sect, considered heretical by orthodox Jews, who broke away from mainstream Judaism in Baghdad in the eighth century CE. Karaites reject the rabbinical interpretation of the scriptural laws and their name, which is connected with the Hebrew word for Scripture, is meant to imply that they recognize only the biblical text itself as authoritative. Although Karaism was at one time a real threat to Judaism, there are probably fewer than 15,000 Karaites in the world today, of whom 7,000 live in Israel. Most of them arrived there from Arab countries after 1948.

Resources List

Books for Further Reading

Non-Fiction
Alpert, C., *Israel* (Minerva)
Cohn, Marta, *Hannah Senesh: Her Life and Diary* (Vallentine Mitchell, London)
Dayan, Moshe, *Story of My Life*
Guiladi, Y., *One Jerusalem* (Keter Publishing House, Jerusalem);
  Fodor's Guide to Israel (Hodder & Stoughton)
Kubie, N.B., *Israel* (Franklin Watts)
Larsen, E., *Israel* (B.T. Batsford)
Levi, A., *Bazak Guide to Israel* (Harper and Row)
Lyle, G., *Let's Visit Israel* (Burke)
Meir, Golda, *My Life* (Futura)
Rutland, J., *Looking at Israel* (A. & C. Black)
Sykes, Christopher, *Cross Roads to Israel, 1917-48* (Indiana, 1973)

Reference
The Bible
Encyclopaedia Judaica (Keter Publishing House, Jerusalem)
Facts About Israel: The Authorized Hand Book to Israel The Ministry of Foreign Affairs,
  Jerusalem)
Israel Pocket Library-Society (Keter Publishing House, Jerusalem)

Fiction
Michener, James, *The Source* (Corgi, 1967)
Reid Banks, Lynne *One More River* (Puffin)
Uris, Leon *Exodus* (Corgi, 1970)

For Further Information

Israel Information Centre,
214 Yaffo Road,
P O Box 13010,
Jerusalem,
Israel

Embassy of Israel,
2 Palace Green,
London
W8 4QB

Jewish National Fund,
Harold Poster House,
Kingsbury Circle,
London,
NW9 9SP

Kibbutz Representatives,
College House,
Finchley Road,
London
NW3

Magen David Adom,
100 Gloucester Place,
London
W1

W.I.Z.O.,
107 Gloucester Place,
London
W1

Index